SIMMONE LOGUE
IN THE
KITCHEN

SIMMONE LOGUE
IN THE KITCHEN

120 FAVOURITE RECIPES FOR
BREAKFASTS, LUNCHES, DINNERS,
PICNICS AND PARTIES

MURDOCH BOOKS

CONTENTS

SO MANY KITCHENS
A LIFE IN THE DAY OF SIMMONE LOGUE

I grew up in a small Australian country town called Muswellbrook, in the Hunter Valley of New South Wales. I had an amazing childhood. My twin sister Joey and I were always off on one adventure or another. If there was a tree with fruit on it, we'd be climbing it. If there was a watering hole or bubbling creek, we'd be in it. Picking, fishing and fossicking, gravitating to the fruits of the land, always so curious about nature and fascinated by what it brought to the table.

Both my grannies were amazing cooks, so it seems only natural that we inherited their interest in all things edible and that a love of food quickly started to flow through our veins.

My Nanna Logue was the cooking teacher at the town's high school, always bringing freshly baked treats home from school, and on weekends working on new recipes to add to her list of favourites. She had an amazing vegetable patch and a chicken coop. As kids we knew exactly where our food came from, and we were intrigued. I have memories of Nanna, huddled down in the vegie patch, taking a big, loud crunchy bite out of the greenest, shiniest capsicum, then passing it over to us kids. We loved retrieving eggs from the chicken coop and learning about animal husbandry. It was Nanna

Logue who taught us how to catch crayfish from the dam, using a piece of chuck steak in the bottom of an old pair of her pantyhose as bait.

My maternal granny, Nanna Fairhurst, immigrated from England with my Pop, who worked in the coal pits in Newcastle, New South Wales. Nanna Fairhurst always had something on the stove; she ran the coal mine canteen and on weekends she would bake cakes and scones to sell there during the week. I have such fond memories of her picking rhubarb from the garden and gently stewing it in her kitchen.

As a child, these experiences must have soaked in, as I have always felt a pull towards all things culinary.

My own career in the kitchen began 25 years ago in my small flat in Sydney's Neutral Bay. I baked my favourite recipes, handed down from my nannas, and would walk the finished goods up a steep hill to sell to local cafe owners. Back then, I had little more than a bowl, a hand mixer, a love of cooking and a dream to sell my cakes to the world. In those early days I did everything myself — baked the cakes, iced the cakes, washed the pans and floors, did the accounts and even delivered the cakes. It was exhausting, but exhilarating.

In time, I bought an oven and a big industrial-scale mixer and rented an old butcher's shop in East Balmain, where I created a range of puddings with accompanying sauces to wholesale to the restaurant and cafe industry, filling a niche in the market — I recognised that many chefs and cafe owners didn't have the time or resources to make their own desserts and needed a 'fairy pudding godmother' to deliver beautiful homemade desserts to the back door. My sticky date puddings with caramel sauce were especially popular, and before long I was employing people to help me. It was wonderful to build my business to a point where I could get some support.

From there, setting up a catering division just seemed a natural thing to do. People were coming into the shop to buy their home dinners, then asking if we could come and cook for them in their own kitchen, and now catering is a huge part of our business. I love cooking in other people's homes; it brings me so much joy to make people happy through the power of beautiful food. The kitchen is my natural habitat — a place where I can 'eat, sleep, breathe' my passion for food.

All these years later, I now have 80 employees, and each week my team and I bake tens of thousands of pies, braise 1000 kilos of beef bourguignon and ice many hundreds of cupcakes. We cook for lunches, dinners, parties and picnics, footy games and airlines. Our days are full of 'foodie inspiration' where we exchange ideas, swap recipes, and share new inspirations. We like to think of our cooking as 'home meal therapy', creating delicious home-style meals for busy people. Handmade, fresh and elegant food, prepared with love and integrity, and based around what we find in the market that week, so the produce is always shining out — fresh, seasonal and relevant. It is a truly magical environment, and I owe a huge part of my success to the wonderful people I have around me. I am lucky because most of my key people have come on the journey from cooking in the back of my small store in Balmain, to the humming 1000 square metre facility we now call home. We have all grown professionally together and continue to, as one big family.

When I decided to write this book, I had no idea how sentimental it would make me feel. Every recipe took me back to somewhere along the way in my journey to becoming a great cook and successful businesswoman. Inspired by my colleagues, friends and family, each recipe in this book has a story of how it came about, or a fond memory of the first time I tasted it and made it my own.

I hope you find within these pages some inspiration and new ideas, or maybe a few new favourite recipes to add to your own collection, passing them down as they have been passed to me, bringing enjoyment to so many.

Happy cooking.

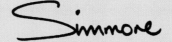

Chapter One

THE TOOLBOX

TO MY MIND, THIS IS THE MOST IMPORTANT
CHAPTER IN THIS BOOK, AS THE RECIPES
WITHIN IT WEAVE ALL THE WAY THROUGH
THE PAGES THAT FOLLOW.

They bring perkiness, piquancy, deliciousness — that special
something that elevates a perfectly lovely dish to a whole new
ethereal and unforgettable level.

The French would define many elements in this chapter as
an 'accoutrement', meaning an accessory item of equipment
or dress. Besides the basic items, such as shortcrust pastry and
béchamel sauce, I like to think of the recipes in this chapter as
the shiny diamonds of my collection — the extra bit of love,
the 'wow' factor, and the full stop that, when added to a dish,
can somehow make it special and complete.

All the recipes in my toolbox have a special place in my heart.
I remember where every recipe came from, where I learned it,
and how many extraordinary ways I have included each one
in my cooking over the years.

For this reason I have placed this chapter at the very beginning
of this book. Read the recipes, use the recipes, love the recipes
and make them your own.

This béchamel recipe is easy as pie. Nutmeg is vital to this classic sauce, but don't be tempted to overdo it, or it will overpower the delicate, subtle flavours of the clove, peppercorns and bay leaves.

BÉCHAMEL SAUCE

MAKES **500 ML (17 FL OZ/2 CUPS)**
PREPARATION **15 MINUTES**   COOKING **15 MINUTES**

2 heaped tablespoons butter
2 heaped tablespoons plain (all-purpose) flour
375 ml (13 fl oz/1½ cups) milk
¼ brown onion, roughly sliced
1 clove
1 fresh bay leaf
pinch of sea salt
pinch of freshly ground black pepper
pinch of freshly grated nutmeg

Melt the butter in a heavy-based saucepan. Stir in the flour until smooth, then stir over medium heat for a couple of minutes, to cook out the raw flour taste.

Meanwhile, in another heavy-based saucepan, combine the milk, onion, clove and bay leaf. Bring to a simmer, then remove from the heat.

Strain the aromatics from the milk, then add the warm milk to the flour mixture. Whisk over medium heat until the sauce thickens; this will take about 10 minutes. Season with the salt, pepper and nutmeg.

TIP: The béchamel can be made ahead of time and stored in the fridge, although you'll need to cover the surface with plastic wrap so it doesn't form a crust. To make the sauce spreadable again, warm it in the microwave for a minute or two, until softened to a good usable consistency. You can also double the recipe if needed; keep the quantity of clove and bay leaf the same.

Homemade mayonnaise always tastes so much better than any commercially prepared version. If you make up a decent amount, it will last for months in the fridge, which is why I've included it in my toolbox.

When you've made up your batch of mayo, you can add herbs such as chives, basil or dill, or flavour hits such as chilli, lime or preserved lemon, to groove up your dishes and help your food sing. These are the notes you want to taste on your palate, to keep things interesting — which is why I recommend using vegetable oil or a very light-tasting olive oil in the mayo, as I find extra virgin olive oil too fruity and overpowering in flavour.

MAYONNAISE

MAKES **500 G (1 LB 2 OZ)**
PREPARATION **20 MINUTES**

2 large free-range egg yolks
1 tablespoon dijon mustard
500 ml (17 fl oz/2 cups) vegetable oil
    or very light olive oil
1 tablespoon white wine vinegar
juice of 1 lemon
ground white pepper, to taste

Place a damp folded cloth on your workbench, then place a medium-sized bowl on top. Add the egg yolks and mustard and whisk to combine, using a hand whisk or electric mixer.

Start adding the oil very slowly, whisking after each addition. If you have a friend to help, that would be great at this point — one person could pour the oil in, while the other whisks and holds the bowl. Once half the oil is combined into the egg yolks, you can add the vinegar, then continue slowly adding the rest of the oil.

Whisk in the lemon juice, then season to taste with sea salt and white pepper. Check you are happy with the seasoning, then transfer to a sterilised jar.

Seal the lid and refrigerate. This mayonnaise will last for a good few months in the fridge.

My executive chef, Adam Wilcox, nailed this recipe about ten years ago, and now we just can't live without it. When we cook it in our production kitchen, we make it in batches of 100 kilos, so I've drilled the recipe down to a more manageable amount. Stored in sterilised jars or containers, it will last for several months. I particularly like it with eggs in the morning.

TOMATO RELISH

MAKES **ABOUT 6 X 500 ML (16 OZ) JARS**
PREPARATION **20 MINUTES**　COOKING **1½ HOURS**

1 tablespoon fennel seeds
1 tablespoon mustard seeds
2 cinnamon sticks
80 ml (2½ fl oz/⅓ cup) vegetable oil
400 g (14 oz/2½ cups) chopped onion
2 garlic cloves, finely chopped
5 fresh bay leaves
250 g (9 oz) caster (superfine) sugar
250 ml (9 fl oz/1 cup) red wine vinegar
100 g (3½ oz) tomato paste
　(concentrated purée)
1.8 litres (62½ fl oz) tomato sugo,
　passata or tinned crushed tomatoes
1 tablespoon sea salt

Place a heavy-based frying pan over medium heat. Add the fennel seeds, mustard seeds and cinnamon sticks and dry roast for a few minutes, or until aromatic. Be careful not to burn the spices, or they will become bitter.

Heat the oil in a heavy-based saucepan, then sauté the onion, garlic, bay leaves and toasted spices over medium heat for about 10 minutes, until the onion is soft and the mixture is fragrant.

Add the sugar and vinegar and cook for about 5 minutes, to reduce a little. Stir in the tomato paste and allow to cook out for a further 5 minutes.

Now add the tomato sugo and simmer for about 1 hour, or until the mixture is rich and fragrant. Season with the salt, and freshly ground black pepper to taste.

Leave to cool slightly, then ladle into sterilised jars and seal. The relish will keep for at least 2 months in the pantry. Refrigerate after opening, and use within 2 weeks.

I created this dressing many years ago to accompany my Couscous salad (page 107). Since then, I've discovered many new and wonderful ways to use it. Try serving the dressing with Moroccan-style lamb cutlets just off the barbecue, or drizzled over roasted baby carrots and beetroot.

TAHINI, YOGHURT & POPPY SEED DRESSING

MAKES **600 ML (21 FL OZ)**
PREPARATION **10 MINUTES**

1 garlic clove, crushed
500 g (1 lb 2 oz/2 cups) Greek-style
   yoghurt
4 tablespoons tahini
1 teaspoon ground cumin
1 tablespoon poppy seeds
1 tablespoon honey
1 teaspoon sea salt
zest and juice of 1 lemon

Combine all the ingredients using a hand whisk, adding a little warm water until a pouring consistency is achieved.

The dressing will keep in a clean airtight jar in the refrigerator for up to 2 weeks.

In ballet school, I met a girl called Annette, whose mum hailed from France. Annette was the most beautiful girl in our class, and was so very French, oozing elegance and charm. Annette taught me this vinaigrette recipe, which made me feel terribly grown up — so French, so chic... I've been using it ever since, and in fact my whole family does too. See the effect one recipe can have on so many people for so many years?

LEMON, GARLIC & DIJON DRESSING

MAKES **250 ML (9 FL OZ/1 CUP)**
PREPARATION **10 MINUTES**

1 tablespoon dijon mustard
juice of 1½ lemons
1 garlic glove, peeled and smashed
1 tablespoon finely chopped parsley
100 ml (3½ fl oz) vegetable oil
100 ml (3½ fl oz) olive oil
1 teaspoon sea salt

In a smallish ceramic bowl, combine the mustard, lemon juice, garlic and parsley. Whisk together using a fork or small hand whisk.

Slowly whisk in the vegetable and olive oils until they are all emulsified. Add the salt and some freshly ground black pepper. Check and adjust the seasoning.

Cover and keep in the refrigerator until required; the dressing will keep for up to 3 months.

TIP: Each night, to the original ceramic bowl, you can just keep adding a little lemon juice, oil and seasoning, and you'll soon get to know exactly how you like your dressing. The garlic clove is there just to infuse the dressing, so if you find the garlic flavour a bit overwhelming, just rub the smashed garlic clove around the inside of your salad bowl rather than adding it to the dressing.

Sweet, hot, sour and salty, this dressing captures the essence of Thailand and really brings the palate alive. It's one of my favourites and I use it in so many ways — it's great for dressing a herby, fragrant Thai-style salad, or drizzled over scallops or prawns that are served on spoons or in betel leaves.

Feel free to play with the different flavour components — fish sauce, chilli and lime juice — to get it just how you like it. I prefer my nam jim a little sweeter than most, but you can adjust the seasoning to suit your taste.

NAM JIM

MAKES **60 ML (2 FL OZ/¼ CUP)**
PREPARATION **10 MINUTES**

1 garlic clove, crushed
2 tablespoons lime juice
2 tablespoons fish sauce
2 tablespoons grated palm sugar
  (jaggery)
1 long red chilli, seeds and membranes
  removed, finely chopped
2 tablespoons finely chopped coriander
  (cilantro) leaves

In a small bowl, mix all the ingredients together until the sugar has dissolved.

The dressing will keep in a clean airtight container in the fridge for a couple of weeks.

*Our chilli jam is very addictive. We pair it with our burritos and corn fritters;
it also goes brilliantly with all manner of Thai and Chinese dishes, such as the
Roasted pork belly on page 99, and as an extra dipping sauce with the Pork and water
chestnut dim sums on page 181.*

CHILLI JAM

MAKES **ABOUT 6 X 500 ML (16 OZ) JARS**
PREPARATION **15 MINUTES**   COOKING **35 MINUTES**

2 tablespoons vegetable oil
250 g (9 oz) red Asian shallots,
   roughly chopped
4 garlic cloves, peeled
6 kaffir lime leaves
2 lemongrass stems, cut into finger
   lengths and bruised
1 kg (2 lb 4 oz) long red chillies,
   stalks removed
1 kg (2 lb 4 oz) sugar
250 ml (9 fl oz/1 cup) lime juice
250 ml (9 fl oz/1 cup) fish sauce
1 tablespoon sea salt

Heat the oil in a large heavy-based saucepan. Add the shallot, garlic, lime leaves and lemongrass and cook over medium heat for 5 minutes, or until aromatic.

Add the whole chillies and sugar and cook, stirring, until the sugar has dissolved. Discard the lime leaves and lemon grass.

Blend using a hand-held stick blender, then continue to cook until the jam thickens and becomes transparent and jewel-like in colour; this will take about 30 minutes.

Season with the lime juice, fish sauce and salt. Leave to cool slightly, then ladle into sterilised jars and seal. Refrigerate after opening. The jam will keep for up to 6 months if handled well; always use a scrupulously clean spoon when dipping into it.

This is my most adored condiment, at work and home alike. We use it as a marinade for seafood and chicken, as a dipping sauce for Vietnamese rolls and dim sum, and as an amazing salad dressing. I deliberated about including it in the book, as it is the one recipe I've created that could probably make me a million dollars one day! My colleagues came up with a new name for it: 'Simmone's Move Over Paul Newman I'm Coming On Through, Put It On Everything Spicy Sauce!' I rather liked that. Here I've given you a recipe to make it in bulk, as I know how much you'll love it, and your friends will want to take some home once they try it. You could most certainly halve the recipe, though.

THAI DRESSING

MAKES **3 LITRES (105 FL OZ/12 CUPS)**; RECIPE CAN EASILY BE HALVED
PREPARATION **30 MINUTES**

1 litre (35 fl oz/4 cups) sweet chilli sauce
500 ml (17 fl oz/2 cups) kecap manis
200 ml (7 fl oz) fish sauce
1 tablespoon sesame oil
500 ml (17 fl oz/2 cups) vegetable oil
500 ml (17 fl oz/2 cups) lemon juice
100 ml (3½ fl oz) mirin
1 lemongrass stem, white part only,
    chopped
1 thumb-sized piece of fresh ginger,
    peeled and chopped
2 garlic cloves, chopped
1 bunch (80 g/2¾ oz) mint, leaves
    picked, stalks discarded
1 bunch (90 g/3¼ oz) coriander
    (cilantro), roots, stalks and leaves
    washed well, then chopped
5 kaffir lime leaves, chopped

Place all the ingredients in a food processor and whiz until smooth.

Pour into sterilised bottles and seal. This dressing can be stored in the pantry at cool room temperature, but should be refrigerated after opening. It will keep for up to 6 months.

My friend and fellow cook, Dominique, taught me this pesto recipe many moons ago. He would cook me lamb cutlets with little baby potatoes, a rocket salad and this mint pesto on the side, and it was always the mint pesto that made the meal so memorable. Whenever I cook lamb now, I always serve this pesto alongside.

MINT PESTO

MAKES **500 G (1 LB 2 OZ)**
PREPARATION **20 MINUTES**

2 bunches (160 g/5½ oz) common
  garden mint (the one with the
  rounded leaves)
150 g (5½ oz) peanuts (see Note),
  toasted
80 g (2¾ oz) parmesan cheese, grated
1 garlic clove, chopped
zest and juice of 1 lemon
2 teaspoons sea salt
½ teaspoon freshly ground black pepper
250 ml (9 fl oz/1 cup) olive oil, plus extra
  for covering the pesto

Submerge the mint in cold water and give it a good wash. Drain the water and pick off the leaves, discarding the woody stalks.

Place the mint leaves in a food processor, along with the peanuts, parmesan, garlic, lemon zest, lemon juice, salt and pepper. Start the processor and slowly pour in the olive oil, blending until the pesto comes together, but is still a bit chunky and not too smooth; this should only take a couple of minutes. Check the seasoning and adjust to taste.

Using a spatula, scrape down the bowl, then spoon the pesto into a sterilised jar. Pour a little more olive oil over the top of the pesto to help preserve it.

If you keep the jar in the fridge, and always top it up with fresh olive oil after each use, this delightful pesto should last for 1 month. Serve with lamb or fish.

NOTE: If there are peanut allergies in the family, use another nut instead, such as macadamias or cashews.

Unexpectedly, this pickle goes brilliantly with fish, which is how it was introduced to me by a clever cook called George Ermer in the days of my restaurant, Logue's Eating House. These days we use it with roasted lamb as well, though I think a generous spoonful on a piece of pan-seared blue eye cod is the bomb. It makes a really lovely gift, too, so I often triple the quantity and make extra jars for the ones I love.

EGGPLANT PICKLE

MAKES **2 X 500 ML (16 OZ) JARS**
PREPARATION **30 MINUTES**   COOKING **25 MINUTES**

vegetable oil, for deep-frying
1 kg (2 lb 4 oz) eggplants (aubergines), diced
4 tablespoons olive oil
1 thumb-sized piece of fresh ginger, peeled and finely chopped
6 coriander (cilantro) roots, washed well and finely chopped
3 garlic cloves, finely chopped
1 tablespoon ground turmeric
2 tablespoons ground cumin
2 tablespoons ground coriander
1 tablespoon sweet paprika
1 teaspoon chilli flakes
140 ml (4½ fl oz) lemon juice (about 2 lemons)
2 teaspoons sea salt

In a heavy-based saucepan, heat about 15 cm (6 inches) of vegetable oil to 180°C (350°F), or until a cube of bread dropped into the oil turns golden brown in 15 seconds. Add the eggplant in batches and cook for 3 minutes, or until golden all over. Drain on paper towel.

In a wok, heat the olive oil, then gently fry the ginger, coriander root, garlic and spices over medium–low heat for 3–5 minutes, or until the flavours mingle and the oil separates out.

Add the eggplant and cook for a further 5 minutes. Now add the lemon juice, salt and some freshly ground black pepper and cook for a further 5 minutes, until all the flavours have combined and the mixture has reduced to a good relish consistency.

Check for seasoning, then ladle the hot pickle into sterilised jars. Seal and store in the pantry; the pickle will keep for up to 12 months. Refrigerate after opening and use within 3 weeks.

The colours of this jam really bring life to a dish when you pop a dollop on top. We love to drizzle it over chicken schnitzel leftovers, bundling it all up into a wrap with avocado, or pairing it with our mini sausage rolls as a dipper.

RED CAPSICUM JAM

MAKES **2 X 500 ML (16 OZ) JARS**
PREPARATION **10 MINUTES**   COOKING **40 MINUTES**

4 tablespoons vegetable oil
2 red capsicums (peppers), roughly chopped
2 red onions, roughly chopped
4 long red chillies, chopped
250 g (9 oz) cherry tomatoes
100 g (3½ oz) sugar
50 ml (1¾ fl oz) fish sauce

Heat the oil in a heavy-based saucepan over medium–high heat. Sauté the capsicum, onion and chilli for 5 minutes, or until softened and slightly caramelised.

Add the tomatoes and cook for 6 minutes, or until soft and translucent.

Add the sugar and the fish sauce and simmer for 30 minutes, until thickened. Leave to cool slightly, then purée using a food processor.

Ladle into sterilised jars and seal. The jam will keep in the pantry for 6–12 months. Refrigerate after opening and use within 1 month.

Preserved lemon has such a unique flavour. Once you start to include it in your cooking, its magic draws you in and you'll find yourself under its intoxicating spell. I use it in tagines, roasts, stuffings, salads, and even in my mayonnaise (page 13) when serving seafood. I love the look of the lemon-filled jars lined up on a shelf in the kitchen, although sadly they are best stored in a dark cupboard, out of the light.

PRESERVED LEMON

MAKES **1 X 2 LITRE (64 OZ) JAR**
PREPARATION **30 MINUTES**   PRESERVING TIME **2 MONTHS**

10 thick-skinned lemons
300 g (10½ oz) sea salt
3 cinnamon sticks, broken
1 tablespoon fennel seeds
1 tablespoon black peppercorns
5 fresh bay leaves
extra lemon juice, for filling the jar
2 tablespoons olive oil

Wash the lemons well, then cut each one into quarters and place in a large bowl.

Place a couple of spoonfuls of the salt in a 2 litre (64 oz) sterilised glass jar, or one that is large enough to hold 10 lemons.

Add the remaining salt to the lemons, along with the cinnamon sticks, fennel seeds, peppercorns and bay leaves. Mix to combine.

Gently press the lemon quarters and aromatics into the jar, with the skin side facing out, and pressing down to extract as much lemon juice as possible. Top with extra lemon juice to cover the lemons, if required, then pour the olive oil over the top.

Seal with a tight-fitting lid and store in a cool dark place for at least 2 months before using.

To use the lemons, always use a clean implement to remove the lemon quarters from the jar. Scrape out and discard the fleshy inner bit. Rinse the rind to wash off the excess salt, then finely chop or cut into thin strips and add it to your recipes. Be sure to reseal the jar properly each time; handled well, your preserved lemons will keep indefinitely.

TIP: If you are a bit impatient like me, you can speed up the process by freezing the lemon quarters for 4 hours in a plastic bag before they're mixed with the salt and spices, then continue with the recipe. Also, if a bit of white mould appears on the lemons, it's harmless, so don't worry — simply rinse it off before using.

LABNEH

MAKES **800 G (1 LB 12 OZ)**
PREPARATION **15 MINUTES + 2 DAYS DRAINING**

1 kg (2 lb 4 oz) creamy Greek-style
   yoghurt
1 teaspoon fine salt
6 thyme sprigs, leaves picked
4 garlic cloves, peeled and cut into
   quarters
2 red bird's eye chillies, halved
   lengthways, seeds intact
1 teaspoon black peppercorns
virgin olive oil, for covering the labneh

Lay a piece of muslin (cheesecloth) in a medium-sized bowl. (Alternatively, you could use two large clean sheets of open-weave cloth, laying the top cloth so the weave is sitting at right angles to the weave in the bottom cloth.)

In a separate bowl, mix together the yoghurt and salt, then tip into the muslin-lined bowl. Gather up the sides of muslin and tie together with a piece of kitchen string. (It's good to have a friend to help at this point — one to gather and hold, and the other to tie the string.)

Place the cloth-wrapped yoghurt in a sieve, then set the sieve over the bowl, so that the whey (the watery liquid component of the yoghurt) will drain down into the bowl. Now put the whole thing in the fridge and forget about it for a while. What you are doing is making yoghurt cheese, and the longer you leave it to drain, the firmer your cheese will become. I like to leave it for 2 days.

After 2 days, discard the whey that has accumulated in the bowl. When you peel away the cloth, you should find that the curd has turned into a soft, creamy cheese. With clean hands, roll the cheese into balls a bit larger than a walnut. Place them back in the bowl, or in a large, sterilised glass preserving jar. Add the thyme, garlic, chilli and peppercorns, then cover the labneh with a good layer of olive oil.

Store in the fridge; the labneh will keep for up to 1 month. Always use a sterilised spoon to retrieve the labneh, and make sure the cheese is always submerged under the oil.

TIP: In the winter months at our country house, we hang the labneh from the oak tree in the backyard. Romantic, huh!

These tomatoes are so handy to have in the fridge to jazz up a pasta dish, top a pizza, or add to a salad to make it a bit special. Sometimes I also add a few smashed garlic cloves to infuse into the olive oil, then use the oil in salad dressings or drizzle it over bruschetta. The most important element of this recipe is the slow oven-roasting. Don't be impatient — time is your best friend here!

EASY OVEN-ROASTED TOMATOES

MAKES **ABOUT 28 PIECES**
PREPARATION **10 MINUTES**   COOKING **2½ HOURS**

2 tablespoons good olive oil, plus extra oil for covering the tomatoes
1 kg (2 lb 4 oz) ripe red roma (plum) or vine-ripened tomatoes
1 tablespoon caster (superfine) sugar
1 small handful of fresh herbs from the garden, such as basil, thyme or oregano

Preheat the oven to 150°C (300°F). Line two baking trays with baking paper, then drizzle each tray with 1 tablespoon of the olive oil.

Cut the tomatoes in half and place them on the baking trays, cut side up. Sprinkle the tomatoes with the sugar, then some sea salt and freshly ground black pepper. Scatter the herbs randomly over the top.

Bake for 2½ hours, or slightly longer if needed, until the tomatoes are darker in colour and slightly dehydrated.

Leave to cool, then transfer to a clean airtight container. Add enough extra olive oil to completely cover the tomatoes, then store in the fridge until required. The tomatoes will keep for several weeks; always use a clean fork or pair of tongs to retrieve these plump little morsels, or the ones remaining in the container will ferment.

We call our veal jus 'liquid gold'. It does take a lot of time and patience to prepare, but it is well worth the effort — it freezes brilliantly and will take your cooking to a whole new level. I often freeze the jus in ice-cube trays, so I can just pop out a cube to enrich a soup, sauce or casserole. Order your veal bones ahead from your local butcher, and ask him to cut them into pieces for you to expose the marrow.

VEAL JUS

MAKES 1.5 LITRES (52 FL OZ/6 CUPS)
PREPARATION 30 MINUTES + OVERNIGHT REFRIGERATION   COOKING 10 HOURS

6 kg (13 lb) veal bones
200 g (7 oz) tomato paste (concentrated purée)
3 brown onions, skins left on, roughly chopped
2 carrots, roughly chopped
2 leeks, washed well and roughly chopped (including the darker green bits)
2 tomatoes, quartered
1 garlic bulb, skin left on, cut in half
6 thyme sprigs
½ bunch (75 g/2½ oz) flat-leaf (Italian) parsley, including the stalks
5 fresh bay leaves
1 tablespoon black peppercorns

Preheat the oven to 180°C (350°F). Line four large baking trays with baking paper. Place the bones on the baking trays and dot with the tomato paste. Working in batches if necessary, roast the bones for 20 minutes, or until nice and golden. Be careful not to burn the bones or your jus will be bitter.

Transfer the roasted bones to a very large stockpot, or two large saucepans if need be. Add the vegetables, garlic and aromatics. Turn the heat to medium, pour in enough cold water to cover the bones, then slowly bring to the boil. Now reduce the heat to a simmer and cook for 8 hours, skimming the scum from the top and adding more water as needed to keep the bones submerged at all times.

Strain the bones and vegetables from the liquid. Leave the stock to cool, then refrigerate overnight.

The next day, discard the fat that has congealed on top of the stock. Pour the stock into a clean heavy-based saucepan. Bring to a simmer and cook for 1–2 hours, or until reduced to one-quarter. Cool, then freeze in ice-cube trays or small plastic containers for future use. The jus can be frozen for up to 1 year.

WONDERFUL WAYS WITH VEAL JUS: Make a red wine sauce by simmering some red wine until reduced by one-quarter, then adding a frozen ice cube or two of veal jus. Or, after roasting chicken, you can make a fabulous gravy by adding a frozen cube of veal jus to the roasting pan, with a squeeze of lemon juice and fresh thyme.

I'm a real stickler for a thin, yeasty pizza dough. I don't want the dough to be the star of the show, rather a carrier for the tasty things on top. I learned this recipe from a pizza chef many years ago and have never forgotten it.

PIZZA DOUGH

MAKES **6 MEDIUM PIZZA BASES**
PREPARATION **25 MINUTES + 1 HOUR RISING**

2 teaspoons dried yeast
1 kg (2 lb 4 oz) strong flour (also labelled '00' flour or 'bread' flour), plus extra for dusting
200 g (7 oz) fine semolina
1 teaspoon cooking salt
1 tablespoon caster (superfine) sugar
4 tablespoons extra virgin olive oil
650 ml (22½ fl oz) lukewarm water

Put the yeast in a small stainless steel bowl. Add enough warm water to get a little slurry going; about 4 tablespoons should do. It is important that the water is not too hot or it will kill the yeast. Leave in a warm place for 5 minutes or so, to let the yeast start activating.

Sift the flour, semolina and salt onto your workbench, then sprinkle with the sugar. Mix the olive oil and water in a jug.

Make a well in the middle of the flour mixture. Pour the yeast mixture and the oil mixture into the well. Using a spoon, gently swirl the liquid into the flour and start to slowly pull the sides of the flour into the well. As more flour combines with the yeast and oil mixture, dust your hands with a little extra flour and start to knead until you get a smooth dough. Knead the dough for a further 5 minutes.

Place the dough in a large bowl that's been dusted with flour, then dust a little more flour over the top. Cover with a tea towel and place in a warm spot for about 1 hour, until the dough has doubled in size.

Place the dough on a floured workbench. Push down on it with your knuckles to remove any large air pockets; this is called 'knocking back' the dough. Now give the dough another gentle knead.

At this stage you can divide the dough into six pieces, roll into balls and place on a floured tray ready to use, or you could wrap the dough in plastic wrap and keep it in the fridge for a day, or in the freezer for up to 3 months.

TIP: If you have frozen the pizza dough, it will need to be thawed in the fridge for a day or overnight before using.

So buttery and short, this pastry works really well with a lovely three-cheese tart, or the classic quiche Lorraine. I learned the recipe from Maggie Beer's cookbooks; I have devoured every word she has ever written! The secret is to make sure the butter is super cold when adding it into the flour, and to give the pastry a good rest after using it to line your pie tin. When making a sweet pie or tart, I just add 1–2 tablespoons sugar to the pastry — a testament to how versatile this recipe is.

SOUR CREAM PASTRY

MAKES **575 G (1 LB 4 OZ)**
PREPARATION **10 MINUTES + 50 MINUTES RESTING**

150 g (5½ oz) chilled salted butter
300 g (10½ oz/2 cups) plain
   (all-purpose) flour, sifted, plus
   extra for dusting
125 g (4½ oz/½ cup) sour cream

Chop the chilled butter into chunks, then place in a food processor with the flour. Pulse until the butter is the size of cherries. Add the sour cream and pulse again, until just incorporated.

Turn out onto a cool, floured surface and form the dough into a rectangle. Cover and leave to rest in the fridge for 20 minutes.

Roll out to the shape and thickness directed in your recipe, then press into your pie or tart tin. Trim the pastry edges, then rest in the fridge again for 30 minutes, before baking and filling according to your recipe instructions.

TIP: The pastry can be wrapped up and frozen for up to 3 months; simply thaw it in the fridge for a day or overnight before using.

Some may say life's too short to make your own puff pastry. To that I say, yes, there are some great ready-made puff pastries on the market, so by all means use them if you're in a hurry — but when you do have the luxury of time, it's well worth giving this recipe a go. It's a bit of a cheat's version of the traditional puff pastry recipe, but the results are still splendiferous.

EASY ROUGH PUFF PASTRY

MAKES **1 KG (2 LB 4 OZ)**
PREPARATION **20 MINUTES + AT LEAST 1 HOUR RESTING**

225 g (8 oz/1½ cups) plain (all-purpose) flour, sifted, plus extra for dusting

225 g (8 oz/1½ cups) self-raising flour, sifted

450 g (1 lb) chilled salted butter, chopped

180 ml (6 fl oz) ice-cold water

Place all the flour on a clean workbench and scatter the chopped butter on top. With a dough scraper, combine the butter and flour until mixed. There should still be bits of butter in the mixture, and it should look really 'raggy'.

Make a well in the centre. Add the cold water, scraping the mixture together to combine. Bring the dough together with your hands. Divide into two equal portions, then form each into a flat disc. Wrap each disc in plastic wrap and rest in the refrigerator for 30 minutes.

Remove the plastic wrap and place the dough on a lightly floured workbench. Roll out each disc into a rectangle measuring about 40 cm x 15 cm (16 inches x 6 inches), and about 1.5 cm (⅝ inch) thick.

Fold in the short ends, to meet in the centre. Now fold in half, to form a book fold.

Roll and fold each piece of dough twice more.

Cover with plastic wrap and rest for at least 30 minutes in the refrigerator, before rolling out and cooking as the recipe directs. Any leftover puff pastry can be rolled up and frozen in plastic wrap for up to 3 months; thaw in the fridge for 24 hours before using.

> *This is the pastry we use in our pies, quiches and tarts. It's also a great one to have stashed away in the freezer for last-minute entertaining; at home, I often use any left-over pastry to line a flan tin, wrap it in plastic and pop it in the freezer, ready to whip up a quick quiche for lunch if people drop around unannounced.*
>
> *Cooking legend Stephanie Alexander has a great tip regarding the butter. She suggests grating your butter into the flour, to make it easier to incorporate — but do make sure your butter is nice and cold, straight from the fridge.*

SHORTCRUST PASTRY

MAKES **500 G (1 LB 2 OZ)**
PREPARATION **15 MINUTES + 1 HOUR RESTING**

300 g (10½ oz/2 cups) plain
    (all-purpose) flour, sifted, plus
    extra for dusting
150 g (5½ oz) chilled salted butter,
    chopped or grated
60 ml (2 fl oz/¼ cup) ice-cold water

Place the sifted flour on your workbench. Scatter the butter over and quickly work it into the flour. Don't worry about lumpy bits. Make a well in the centre and add the water. With the palm of your hand, quickly work the pastry together, by pushing the dough into the workbench away from you in a sweeping movement. Gather the dough together, shaping it into a flat ball. Dust with a little extra flour, wrap in plastic wrap, then rest in the refrigerator for 30 minutes.

Roll out to the shape and thickness directed in your recipe, then press into your pie or tart tin. Trim the pastry edges, then rest in the refrigerator again for 30 minutes, before baking and filling according to your recipe instructions.

The pastry can be made 3–5 days in advance; cover with plastic wrap and keep in the fridge. It can also be frozen for up to 3 months; simply thaw it in the fridge for 24 hours before using.

VARIATION: For the chia seed pastry on page 162, add 3 tablespoons chia seeds to the flour before working the butter in.

Here's a great recipe if you need a shortcrust for a sweet pie or flan. It works a treat in the Chocolate ganache tart on page 205.

SWEET ALMOND SHORTCRUST PASTRY

MAKES **620 G (1 LB 6 OZ)**
PREPARATION **15 MINUTES + 30 MINUTES RESTING**

125 g (4½ oz) unsalted butter, softened
125 g (4½ oz) sugar
½ teaspoon vanilla extract
2 free-range eggs
200 g (7 oz/1⅓ cups) plain
   (all-purpose) flour
50 g (1¾ oz/½ cup) almond meal

Using an electric stand mixer fitted with the paddle attachment, beat the butter, sugar and vanilla until light and creamy. Add the eggs one at a time until incorporated.

Sift the flour, then gently mix it through. Finally, add the almond meal and mix to combine.

Turn the dough out onto your workbench and shape it into a flat disc. Cover with plastic wrap and rest in the refrigerator for 30 minutes, before rolling out and using as directed in your recipe.

The pastry can be made 3–5 days in advance: cover with plastic wrap and keep in the fridge. It can also be frozen for up to 3 months; simply thaw it in the fridge for 24 hours before using.

'Beware the sourdough,' warns my brother Andy, who gave me this recipe. *'Once you get started, you don't own it, it owns YOU!'* This is because to make a good sourdough bread, you first need to get yourself a starter culture. For this, you need three simple ingredients: flour, water and time. LOTS of time, because you'll need to feed the starter culture every day for a week before it will be ready to use in your sourdough. (A tip from Andy: use good organic, unbleached plain wheat flour and filtered water — most tap waters contain chlorine, which will affect the wellbeing of the good bacteria you need to keep your starter thriving and happy.)

I've written this recipe for two loaves as it freezes so well, but you could halve or double it. Once you've mastered it, groove it up by adding fruit, nuts, garlic, herbs, olives...

SOURDOUGH BREAD

MAKES **2 LOAVES**
PREPARATION **2 HOURS + 7 DAYS FERMENTING + 1 DAY STRENTHENING**
PROVING **18 HOURS**   BAKING **50 MINUTES**

STARTER CULTURE

organic unbleached plain (all-purpose)
   flour
filtered water
½ teaspoon honey (optional)

TO MAKE THE STARTER CULTURE

In a clean container, whisk 35 g (1¼ oz/¼ cup) flour with 60 ml (2 fl oz/¼ cup) filtered water. Don't worry too much about lumps — Andy says they are good! Cover with a tea towel and leave to rest on your kitchen bench for 12 hours.

After 12 hours, add 75 g (2½ oz/½ cup) flour and 80 ml (2½ fl oz/⅓ cup) water every day for 1 week. It's important to whisk each new addition in well, to aerate the starter as much as possible; this ensures the bacteria needed to ferment the new flour is evenly distributed and can do its job. Also, when you add the new flour and water each day, make sure your container is only half full of the starter mixture — you may need to discard some, to allow the starter to keep growing and not expand past the capacity of your container. If there isn't much action, try feeding the starter by adding the honey to move things along.

After 1 week, you should have a really bubbling, strong and robust starter, with a lovely clean, sour aroma. At this stage it will keep indefinitely in an airtight container in the fridge. If a watery slurry develops on top, just scoop it off as it is harmless; it may be a result of adding a little too much water when feeding the starter.

A DAY BEFORE BAKING: STRENGTHEN THE STARTER

The day before you want to bake your loaf, you'll need to feed your starter three times to build up its strength. Take 100 g (3½ oz) of the starter (discard the rest) and add 50 g (1¾ oz/⅓ cup) flour and 50 ml (1¾ fl oz) filtered water. After 8 hours, add another 100 g (3½ oz/⅔ cup) flour and 100 ml (3½ fl oz) filtered water. After a further 8 hours, add a final 200 g (7 oz/1⅓ cups) flour and 200 ml (7 fl oz) filtered water. You should now have about 800 g (1 lb 12 oz) strengthened starter culture for your loaf. Follow the recipe below and hold back the remaining starter culture for future breadmaking, keeping it in the fridge and feeding it again the day before using.

TO PROVE AND BAKE YOUR LOAVES

Fit the paddle attachment to an electric stand mixer. Add all the bread ingredients to the mixer bowl and mix at medium speed for 13 minutes. Transfer the dough to a clean, oiled bowl, cover with plastic wrap and leave to rest at room temperature for 20 minutes.

Turn the dough out onto your work bench. Fold by pulling each corner of the dough into the centre once, then turn the loaf seam side down. Place back in the bowl, cover again with plastic wrap and rest for 2 hours.

Turn the dough out onto your workbench and cut into two even pieces, about 400 g (14 oz) each. Fold again as before. Lay the loaves on an oiled tray, cover with plastic wrap and rest for 30 minutes.

Take each loaf and fold again. This time, turn them seam side down onto an oiled, heavy-based baking tray. Prove in the refrigerator for a final 14–16 hours.

Preheat the oven to 200°C (400°F). Using a sharp knife or razor blade, cut diagonal slashes across the loaves, about one-quarter of the way into the dough. Bake for 40–50 minutes, or until the loaves sound hollow when tapped on the base. Leave to cool, then store in a bread bin, or wrap and freeze for later enjoyment.

TO STRENGTHEN THE STARTER

100 g (3½ oz) starter culture
 (see opposite)
350 g (12 oz/2⅓ cups) organic
 unbleached plain (all-purpose) flour
350 ml (12 fl oz) filtered warm water

FOR THE BREAD

200 g (7 oz) strengthened starter culture
330 g (11½ oz/2¼ cups) organic
 unbleached plain (all-purpose) flour
200 ml (7 fl oz) filtered warm water
50 g (1¾ oz) fine semolina
2 teaspoons salt

This jam is particularly delicious made with ripe summer strawberries at their height of sweetness. We always have it on our breakfast table, and I love using it in our Victoria sponge (page 220). We also serve it with our sourdough toast in our stores, and dab it on petite scones when we are preparing a high tea.

STRAWBERRY JAM

MAKES **ABOUT 4 X 200 ML (6 OZ) JARS**
PREPARATION **15 MINUTES + OVERNIGHT STEEPING**   COOKING **20 MINUTES**

500 g (1 lb 2 oz) strawberries, hulled
375 g (13 oz/1⅔ cups) caster (superfine)
   sugar
zest and juice of 1 lemon

Place the strawberries in a bowl with the sugar and toss. Cover and leave to macerate at room temperature overnight.

Place the strawberry mixture in a saucepan and add the lemon zest and juice. Cook very gently over low heat for 5 minutes, or until the sugar has dissolved.

Now turn the heat up and cook on a rolling boil for 15 minutes, or until the mixture has reached setting point. To check the jam has reached setting point, spoon a little jam onto a saucer that has been chilled in the freezer for about 5 minutes. Leave the jam for 15–20 seconds, then run your finger through it. If the jam is ready, it will wrinkle and feel sticky. If it doesn't, keep cooking the mixture a while longer.

Skim the scum from the top, then leave to settle and cool for about 10 minutes before ladling into sterilised jars. Seal and keep in a cool, dark place; the jam will keep for up to 1 year. Once opened, store in the refrigerator and use within 3 months.

> *Many years ago, a colleague brought in a jar of blood orange marmalade that her granny had made. I'll never forget it — it was the colour of rubies and the taste was sublime. Ever since, I've visited the markets every August to buy 100 kilos of blood oranges to make our yearly batch. I have never been able to quite get the clarity of colour I saw in the jar that day, although I've come pretty close. The important part is the double boiling and discarding the water, as this removes a lot of the bitterness from the oranges.*
>
> *In our stores we serve this jam with our sourdough, as well as in jars as a 'grab and go' item; at home we always have a jar on our breakfast table. It goes beautifully with my Rustic farmhouse pâté (page 74) on toast, garnished with fresh thyme.*

BLOOD ORANGE MARMALADE

MAKES **4 X 250 ML (8 OZ) JARS**
PREPARATION **30 MINUTES**   COOKING **1 HOUR**

1 kg (2 lb 4 oz) blood oranges (pick the ones with the most colour in them)
1 kg (2 lb 4 oz) caster (superfine) sugar
125 ml (4 fl oz/½ cup) lemon juice

Place the whole oranges in a large saucepan and cover with cold water. Bring to the boil, then drain off the water.

Cover the oranges with more cold water, bring to the boil once more, then drain again.

When the oranges are cool enough to handle, cut them in half and remove the seeds. Cut the oranges into thin strips and place in a saucepan, along with any precious juices that gathered on your chopping board. Stir in the sugar and lemon juice.

Cook over medium heat for 30 minutes, or until a teaspoon of the mixture placed on a cold saucer from the fridge sets like jelly. If the pectin hasn't gelled within this time, you can help it along by whizzing the mixture up a tiny bit with a hand-held stick blender. You don't want to cook the marmalade for too long, or the sugar will start to caramelise and you'll lose that lovely ruby-coloured clarity.

Ladle the hot marmalade into sterilised jars. Seal and store in a dark cupboard; the marmalade should last for a couple of years. Once opened, store in the refrigerator and use within 3 months.

> *When we were growing up, lemon curd used to be sold in jars at the local show each year, and there'd be keen competition among the ladies in the Country Women's Association as to whose was best. I still have fond memories of eating lemon curd on toast, although you could also serve it for breakfast on French toast, with a bit of fresh passionfruit stirred through (see page 56); it's also great on cheesecake (page 210), swirled through a soft meringue roll, dolloped on scones, or as a filling in a vanilla butterfly cake. It lasts for months in a sterilised jar in the fridge; you could also double or triple the recipe to make a good batch to give as gifts.*

LEMON CURD

MAKES **1 X 500 ML (16 OZ) JAR**
PREPARATION **10 MINUTES**   COOKING **15 MINUTES**

250 g (9 oz) unsalted butter
zest of 2 lemons, plus the juice of
   3 lemons
3 large free-range egg yolks
190 g (6¾ oz) caster (superfine) sugar

Put the butter and lemon zest in a heavy-based saucepan and place over medium heat.

In a separate bowl, whisk together the egg yolks and sugar.

When the butter has melted, add the egg yolk mixture and lemon juice, then whisk constantly over medium heat until the curd thickens. This will take about 10 minutes.

Leave to cool, then ladle into a sterilised jar and seal. The curd will keep for at least 2 months in the fridge.

> *I tend to use frangipane a lot in autumn, as it marries beautifully with autumn fruits such as pear; another divine thing to do is to use it as a filling for a tart and top it with prunes that have been soaked overnight in Cognac or Armagnac (see page 199), or berries, figs or any fruit that is in season. In the stores on weekends, I also dip freshly made croissants in sugar syrup, fill them with frangipane, then sprinkle them with slivered almonds. Hot out of the oven, they are seriously delicious!*

FRANGIPANE

MAKES **650 G (1 LB 7 OZ)**
PREPARATION **15 MINUTES**

150 g (5½ oz) butter, softened
150 g (5½ oz/⅔ cup) caster (superfine) sugar
1 teaspoon vanilla extract
2 large free-range eggs
180 g (6 oz/1¾ cups) almond meal
2 tablespoons cornflour (cornstarch)

Using an electric mixer, beat the butter, sugar and vanilla until light and creamy. Add the eggs and beat until combined.

Fold in the almond meal and cornflour and gently combine.

Store the frangipane in an airtight container in the fridge, where it will keep for several weeks.

BUTTER CREAM

MAKES **850 G (1 LB 14 OZ/5½ CUPS)**
PREPARATION **15 MINUTES**

250 g (9 oz) unsalted butter, softened
500 g (1 lb 2 oz/4 cups) icing
    (confectioners') sugar, sifted
2 teaspoons vanilla extract
80 ml (2½ fl oz/⅓ cup) thin (pouring/
    whipping) cream

Using an electric mixer, whip the butter until light and fluffy. Add the icing sugar and vanilla and whip for 3 minutes. Now add the cream and whip for a further 2 minutes, or until your butter cream is light and dreamy and crying out to be swirled on top of cute, buttery cupcakes.

If you are not using it straightaway, cover the butter cream and store in the fridge, where it will keep for several weeks. Let it soften and come to room temperature, then whip it again just before using.

TIP: This heavenly cream is what we use to top our cupcakes, and some of our sponges as well. We vary the colour and flavour by adding ingredients such as coffee, lemon, passionfruit, chocolate, strawberry jam and kaffir lime zest.

CREAM CHEESE ICING

MAKES **300 G (10½ OZ)**
PREPARATION **15 MINUTES**

60 g (2¼ oz/¼ cup) cream cheese,
    softened
30 g (1 oz) salted butter, softened
½ teaspoon vanilla extract
125 g (4½ oz/1 cup) icing (confectioners')
    sugar, sifted
1 tablespoon lemon juice

Using an electric mixer, beat the cream cheese until soft and smooth. Add the butter and vanilla and beat until incorporated. Add the icing sugar and lemon juice and beat until combined.

Scrape down the side of the bowl, cover with plastic wrap and store in the fridge until required. It will keep for several weeks. You'll need to beat it again at room temperature just before using.

TIP: I fell in love with this icing the first time I made Hummingbird cake (page 213). So light, so lovely, and spiked with lemon juice, it complements the cake beautifully. We now make this icing in huge quantities for our stores. From little things, big things grow.

Chapter Two

BREAKFAST

I LOVE BREAKFAST TIME. IT'S WHEN I'M
MOST HUNGRY AND KNOW I NEED TO FUEL
UP TO GET THROUGH A BUSY DAY.

Call me crazy, but I especially love cooking the Saturday
morning brekkie shift in my Double Bay store, seeing customers
coming in all sleepy-eyed and in need of a pick-me-up.

The success of the day depends on being well prepared. In our
business this is called *mise en place*, French for 'putting in place'.
We pump up the classical tunes, use only the freshest free-range
eggs and local sourdough, fill our ovens with buttery croissants
and fruity muffins and roast enough field mushrooms and
tomatoes to set us up for the day. It can get pretty hairy,
so we need to have our heads on straight, roller skates on
and our wits about us.

Here are some of my morning favourites from over 20 years of
brekkie shifts.

BACON & EGG PIE

SERVES **8**
PREPARATION **30 MINUTES**   COOKING **50 MINUTES**

---

plain (all-purpose) flour, for dusting
1 quantity Shortcrust pastry (Toolbox, page 36)
4 tablespoons olive oil
4 red onions, thinly sliced
2 fresh bay leaves
2 tablespoons balsamic vinegar
4 tablespoons tomato paste (concentrated purée)
4 bacon rashers, rind removed, roughly chopped
4 large free-range eggs
250 ml (9 fl oz/1 cup) thin (pouring/ whipping) cream
2 large tomatoes, sliced
50 g (1¾ oz/½ cup) grated cheddar cheese
2 tablespoons chopped flat-leaf (Italian) parsley

Preheat the oven to 180°C (350°F). Grease a 38 cm x 26 cm (15 inch x 10½ inch) baking tray.

On a lightly floured workbench, roll the pastry out to 5 mm (¼ inch) thick, then carefully place it on the baking tray, crimping the edges up around the sides of the tray. It's important the sides are sound, for the pastry to hold the filling. Cover the pastry with a sheet of baking paper and fill with baking beads or uncooked rice or dried beans.

Blind bake the pastry for 10 minutes, then remove the baking beads or rice and bake for a further 10 minutes, or until the pastry is a nice golden colour. Remove from the oven and leave to cool slightly. Turn the oven temperature down to 170°C (325°F).

While the pastry is baking, heat the olive oil in a large frying pan and sauté the onion and bay leaves over medium heat for 10 minutes, or until the onion has softened and the mixture is fragrant. Add the vinegar, season with sea salt and freshly ground black pepper and cook for 5 minutes more. Remove from the heat and leave to cool slightly.

Spread the tomato paste over the cooled pastry base, then top with the sautéed onion mixture. Scatter the chopped bacon over the top. Whisk the eggs and cream together, season with salt and pepper, then pour over the pie. Arrange the tomato slices on top, scatter the cheese over and sprinkle with the parsley. Bake for 30 minutes, or until the egg mixture is golden and set.

Serve warm or cold; the pie will keep in the fridge for up to 5 days.

Each morning, we pull these muffins fresh out of the oven, blueberries glistening, the mellow aroma of baked banana and sugar filling the store. The muffin platter lives up on the counter, right next to the coffee machine. Sometimes that's all you need to perk you up in the morning — a strong coffee and one of these dreamy muffins.

FRUITY BREAKFAST BLUEBERRY & BANANA MUFFINS

MAKES **12 LARGE** OR **24 SMALL MUFFINS**
PREPARATION **20 MINUTES**   BAKING **40 MINUTES**

4 ripe bananas (about 400 g/14 oz)
150 g (5½ oz) light brown sugar
150 g (5½ oz/⅔ cup) caster (superfine) sugar
3 large free-range eggs
300 ml (10½ fl oz) vegetable oil
2 tablespoons sour cream
400 g (14 oz/2⅔ cups) plain (all-purpose) flour
1 teaspoon baking powder
1 teaspoon bicarbonate of soda (baking soda)
pinch of sea salt
150 g (5½ oz/1 cup) fresh or frozen blueberries
100 g (3½ oz) dried banana chips
100 g (3½ oz) raw (demerara) sugar, for sprinkling

Preheat the oven to 180°C (350°F). Line a standard 12-hole muffin tin, or a 24-hole mini muffin tin, with paper cases and lightly spray them with vegetable oil.

Mash the bananas in a bowl. Add the brown sugar, caster sugar, eggs, vegetable oil and sour cream. Using a large spoon, gently mix until combined.

Sift the flour, baking powder, bicarbonate of soda and salt together, then add to the banana mixture and mix for 1 minute, or until well combined. Do not overmix at this stage, or your muffins will lose their light texture.

Spoon the mixture into the muffin cases, then top with the blueberries and banana chips. Sprinkle with the raw sugar.

Bake the large muffins for about 40 minutes, and small muffins for about 20 minutes, or until a skewer inserted into the middle of a muffin comes out clean.

I wondered if these rolls were a bit too simple to include in this book — but we do make at least 500 of these a week across our two stores, so it seemed only right to let you in on my secret, as they are so incredibly yummy and simple to prepare. If you are feeling a bit fuzzy from over-indulging the night before, I promise this will make everything better, so here goes.

BACON & EGG ROLLS WITH AÏOLI & TOMATO RELISH

MAKES **6**
PREPARATION **15 MINUTES** COOKING **20 MINUTES**

6 bacon rashers, rind removed
6 soft sourdough rolls
1 tablespoon butter
1 tablespoon olive oil
6 large free-range eggs
½ garlic clove, crushed
60 g (2¼ oz/¼ cup) Mayonnaise (Toolbox, page 13)
6 tablespoons Tomato relish (Toolbox, page 14)

Preheat the oven to 180°C (350°F). Line a small baking tray with baking paper. Lay the bacon on the tray and bake for 20 minutes, or until the bacon is nice and crispy. During the last 5 minutes, pop the sourdough rolls in the oven to warm through.

Meanwhile, in a frying pan large enough to cook six eggs, heat the butter and olive oil until the butter is foaming. Crack the eggs in and cook over medium heat for 2 minutes, or until done to your liking.

To make the aïoli, mix the garlic into the mayonnaise, then check the seasoning and adjust as needed.

Cut the warm rolls horizontally, almost all the way through, and open them up. Spread both sides with the aïoli. Place one piece of bacon and one egg in each roll. Top with a dollop of tomato relish and a good grind of black pepper. Close up the rolls and serve.

Back in the 1970s, my mum used to make this fruit compote in her crockpot as a dessert for a classy dinner party. Sometimes in the store, when I'm serving it up with our creamy porridge, I close my eyes and suddenly I'm 10 years old again! This recipe makes a large amount of compote, but it lasts for months in the fridge in an airtight container for many later indulgences. You can halve the recipe if you like.

FRUIT COMPOTE WITH CREAMY PORRIDGE & CINNAMON

SERVES 6, WITH LOTS OF LEFTOVER COMPOTE
PREPARATION 15 MINUTES   COOKING 1 HOUR

COMPOTE

600 g (1 lb 5 oz) caster (superfine) sugar
300 ml (10½ fl oz) apple juice
3 cinnamon sticks
3 star anise
peel of 1 lemon, without any bitter
   white pith
200 g (7 oz/1 cup) pitted prunes
200 g (7 oz/1¼ cups) dried apricots
200 g (7 oz/1⅓ cups) dried peaches,
   cut in half
200 g (7 oz/2 cups) dried apples,
   cut in half

PORRIDGE

200 g (7 oz/2 cups) rolled (porridge)
   oats
1 litre (35 fl oz/4 cups) full-cream milk
1 whole nutmeg

To make the compote, place the sugar, apple juice, cinnamon sticks, star anise and lemon peel in a flameproof casserole dish. Add 550 ml (19 fl oz) water and bring to a gentle simmer, stirring to dissolve the sugar. Add all the fruit and cook slowly for 1 hour or so, until the fruit is plump and fragrant and the syrup has a nice viscosity. Serve warm or cold; store the leftovers in an airtight container in the fridge.

To make the porridge, place the oats and milk in a saucepan and cook over medium heat for 10 minutes, stirring occasionally.

To serve, spoon the porridge into six small warmed bowls. Top with the fruit compote and a fresh grating of nutmeg. I like my porridge hot and my compote cold; it's also lovely with a little drizzle of fresh cream.

Not just one of the prettiest breakfast dishes ever, this French toast is also luciously delicious and an ingenious way to use up left-over sourdough. Putting slightly stale bread to such exquisite use always gives me a good feeling, and my customers love it too. Instead of the passionfruit curd, you could drizzle the toasts with maple syrup and top with a scattering of blueberries or sliced banana.

FRENCH TOAST WITH PASSIONFRUIT CURD & ROSE PETALS

SERVES **4**
PREPARATION **20 MINUTES**   COOKING **10 MINUTES**

4 free-range eggs
250 ml (9 fl oz/1 cup) thin (pouring/
    whipping) cream
½ teaspoon vanilla extract
4 tablespoons caster (superfine) sugar
1 tablespoon ground cinnamon
pulp of 2 passionfruit
125 ml (4 fl oz/½ cup) Lemon curd
    (Toolbox, page 44)
8 thick slices Sourdough bread (Toolbox,
    page 38, or use store-bought), about
    4 cm (1½ inches) thick
4 tablespoons vegetable oil
4 tablespoons butter
unsprayed rose petals, to garnish
    (optional)

In a bowl, whisk together the eggs, cream and vanilla. On a large plate, mix together the caster sugar and cinnamon.

Gently fold the passionfruit pulp into the lemon curd. Cut each slice of bread into two pieces.

Place a large frying pan over high heat. Add half the vegetable oil and half the butter and warm until the butter starts to foam. Turn the heat down to medium.

Dip half the bread slices in the egg custard mixture and cook for 2 minutes, or until golden underneath. Turn the slices over and cook the other side. Drain on paper towel, then toss the slices in the cinnamon sugar.

Clean out the pan and repeat with the remaining oil, butter, custard and bread. Meanwhile, heat four plates.

Stack four pieces of toast on each plate. Spoon the passionfruit curd over the top, scatter with rose petals, if using, and enjoy straightaway.

ROASTED FIELD MUSHROOMS WITH SPINACH, LABNEH & SOURDOUGH

SERVES 4
PREPARATION **20 MINUTES**   BAKING **15 MINUTES**

4 large field mushrooms
100 g (3½ oz) salted butter, approximately
4–6 thyme sprigs, leaves picked
1 garlic clove, finely chopped
2 tablespoons balsamic vinegar
1 sourdough batard
200 g (7 oz) baby English spinach leaves
juice of ½ lemon, plus extra lemon wedges to serve
200 g (7 oz) Labneh (Toolbox, page 28)
extra virgin olive oil, for drizzling
chopped flat-leaf (Italian) parsley, for sprinkling

Preheat the oven to 180°C (350°F). Find a baking tray large enough to fit all the mushrooms and line it with baking paper.

Lay the mushrooms on the baking tray, cup side up. Dot a heaped teaspoon of the butter on each. Scatter with the thyme and garlic, drizzle with the vinegar and season with sea salt and freshly ground black pepper.

Bake for 10–15 minutes, or until the mushrooms have softened down and the butter and vinegar have oozed into the mushrooms.

Meanwhile, using a serrated knife, cut the sourdough on a diagonal to give eight good, thick slices. Toast the sourdough slices, smear them with lashings of the remaining butter and keep warm.

In a frying pan, heat 1 tablespoon butter over medium–high heat until it foams. Add the spinach and let it wilt down. Sprinkle with the lemon juice and season with salt and pepper.

Heat four plates and divide the buttered toasts among them. Evenly distribute the spinach among the plates. Top each one with a mushroom, being careful to retain the juices that have gathered in the mushroom cups — it's really good stuff!

Top each with some labneh and a drizzle of extra virgin olive oil. Sprinkle with chopped parsley and serve with lemon wedges.

> *To my mind there is nothing more comforting than the smell of just-baked banana bread wafting through the house on the weekend. Sometimes when I'm on the Saturday morning brekkie shift, I treat myself to a piece of this walnut-studded beauty, toasted with lashings of butter. Just one of the perks of the job, really.*
>
> *We serve our banana bread with the freshest ricotta we can find and a generous drizzle of local honey. The walnuts add a lovely rustic look and a yummy crunch, although they could be omitted or replaced with another nut if you like.*

BANANA BREAD WITH RICOTTA & HONEY

MAKES **1 LOAF**
PREPARATION **20 MINUTES**   BAKING **40 MINUTES**

120 g (4¼ oz) unsalted butter, softened
1 teaspoon vanilla extract
130 g (4½ oz) caster (superfine) sugar
1 tablespoon light brown sugar
2 large free-range eggs
50 ml (1¾ fl oz) milk
4 super-ripe bananas (about 400 g/
   14 oz), mashed
60 g (2¼ oz/½ cup) chopped walnuts,
   plus extra for decorating the loaf
380 g (13½ oz/2½ cups) plain
   (all-purpose) flour
1 teaspoon bicarbonate of soda
   (baking soda)
1½ teaspoons baking powder
pinch of sea salt
fresh ricotta and runny honey, to serve

Preheat the oven to 160°C (315°F). Grease a 23 x 7 cm (9 x 2¾ inch) loaf (bar) tin.

Cream together the butter, vanilla and all the sugar, using an electric mixer. Add the eggs one at a time. Fold in the milk, bananas and chopped walnuts.

Sift together the flour, bicarbonate of soda, baking powder and salt, then gently fold through the mixture.

Pour the mixture into the loaf tin, then scatter with some extra chopped walnuts. Bake for 40 minutes, or until a skewer inserted into the middle of the loaf comes out clean.

Serve plain or toasted, either with a dollop of fresh ricotta and a drizzle of good honey, or just with lashings of butter.

The banana bread will keep for up to 5 days in a bread bin, but also freezes beautifully; wrap it well, freeze it whole, and then thaw it in the fridge for 24 hours before using.

I am very fussy about scrambled eggs. The first thing I do when I employ a new chef is give them a lesson in scrambling eggs.

Scrambled eggs should always be made using two-thirds cream to egg, and should never be 'scrambled', but rather gently pulled and folded, in more of a soft omelette kind of way.

Served on soft sourdough with a perky dill mayo, these quick and easy rolls make for a silky, smoky start to the day.

SMOKED SALMON & SCRAMBLED EGG ROLLS WITH DILL MAYONNAISE

SERVES **4**
PREPARATION **10 MINUTES**   COOKING **10 MINUTES**

4 soft sourdough rolls
2 tablespoons Mayonnaise (Toolbox, page 13)
1 tablespoon finely chopped fresh dill
1 lemon or lime, cut into wedges
6 free-range eggs
200 ml (7 fl oz) thin (pouring/whipping) cream
1 tablespoon butter
8 slices smoked salmon

Preheat the oven to 160°C (315°F). Place the bread rolls on a baking tray and into the oven for 5 minutes to warm through.

Meanwhile, in a small bowl, mix together the mayonnaise, dill and a squeeze of a lemon wedge, then check the seasoning.

In another bowl, whisk together the eggs and cream. Season with sea salt and freshly ground black pepper.

Heat the butter in a non-stick frying pan over medium–high heat until foaming. Add the egg mixture and cook for 30 seconds. With a soft spatula, gently pull the egg mix from the side of the pan and tilt the pan, so the runny bits run into the spaces created. Gently pull and fold the mix. Continue until the egg has just set, and no really runny bits remain; this should take no longer than 1½–2 minutes. Remove from the heat and set aside.

Using a serrated knife, cut the rolls horizontally, but not all the way through. Open the rolls out and smear the dill mayonnaise on each cut side. Top each roll with the scrambled egg and add two smoked salmon slices. Close the rolls up and serve straightaway, with the remaining lemon wedges on the side.

We joke at work about how bad these French-inspired ham and cheese toasties must be for our cholesterol levels, although we believe life is too short to deny ourselves — and our customers agree! Sometimes at home, when we've got the munchies late at night, I whip these up for a bit of 'in front of the telly' snack action.

'CROQUE SIMMONE' WITH FRIED EGG & TOMATO RELISH

SERVES **4**
PREPARATION **20 MINUTES**   COOKING **20 MINUTES**

1 sourdough batard
1 tablespoon dijon mustard
8 slices smoked leg ham
200 g (7 oz/2 cups) grated gruyère cheese
4 tablespoons Béchamel sauce (Toolbox, page 12)
125 ml (4 fl oz/½ cup) thin (pouring/whipping) cream
6 free-range eggs
3 tablespoons olive oil
3 tablespoons butter
4 tablespoons Tomato relish (Toolbox, page 14)

Preheat the oven to 160°C (315°F). Line a baking tray with baking paper.

Using a serrated knife, cut the sourdough on a diagonal to give at least eight thick slices. Lay four bread slices on the workbench, then smear some mustard over each. On each, lay two slices of ham, then sprinkle with the cheese. Season with sea salt and freshly ground black pepper, top with the remaining bread slices, then smear 1 tablespoon of béchamel sauce on each. Sandwich the two parts together, béchamel side down.

In a shallow bowl, mix together the cream and two of the eggs. In a frying pan large enough to hold two sandwiches at a time, heat 1 tablespoon of the oil and 1 tablespoon of the butter, until the butter starts to foam. Dip two sandwiches completely into the egg mixture and lay them in the pan. Cook over medium heat for 1 minute, or until golden underneath, then turn to cook the other side. Drain on paper towel.

Clean out the pan. Heat another 1 tablespoon oil and 1 tablespoon butter in the pan, then fry the remaining two sandwiches in the same way. Place all the sandwiches on the baking tray and bake for 15 minutes, or until the cheese oozes out.

Meanwhile, heat the remaining oil and butter in a clean frying pan over medium heat. Fry the remaining four eggs for 2 minutes, until the white is cooked, but the yolks are still soft and oozy.

Serve the croques on warm plates, topped with a fried egg and a good dollop of tomato relish.

BEAN GUMBO IN TORTILLAS WITH FRIED EGGS & AVOCADO MASH

SERVES 6, WITH PLENTY OF GUMBO LEFTOVER FOR FREEZING
PREPARATION 45 MINUTES   COOKING 1¾ HOURS   BAKING 15 MINUTES

BEAN GUMBO

1 tablespoon chopped coriander (cilantro) root

1 tablespoon chopped fresh ginger

2 garlic cloves, peeled

4 tablespoons vegetable oil

3 cinnamon sticks

3 star anise

4 fresh bay leaves

1 tablespoon ground cumin

1 tablespoon ground coriander

1 tablespoon sweet smoked paprika

¼ teaspoon chilli powder

2 large brown onions, diced

2 carrots, diced

2 red capsicums (peppers), diced

3 celery stalks, diced

2 tablespoons tomato paste (concentrated purée)

2 x 400 g (14 oz) tins chopped tomatoes

2 x 400 g (14 oz) tins red kidney beans, drained and rinsed

500 ml (17 fl oz/2 cups) vegetable stock

1 tablespoon sugar

2 teaspoons sea salt

1 teaspoon freshly cracked black pepper

1 bunch (90 g/3¼ oz) coriander (cilantro), leaves and stalks washed and chopped

1 bunch (80 g/2¾ oz) mint, leaves picked and chopped

FOR THE BEAN GUMBO

Using a mortar and pestle, grind the coriander root, ginger and garlic to a paste.

Heat the oil in a large heavy-based saucepan over medium heat. Fry the coriander, ginger and garlic paste for 3 minutes, or until aromatic.

Add the cinnamon sticks, star anise, bay leaves and ground spices and cook, stirring, for 5 minutes. Keep the heat at medium, as you want the spices to become fragrant, but not burn, or they will become bitter.

Add the diced vegetables and cook for 5 minutes, until they are a little softened. Stir in the tomato paste and cook for 1 minute.

Stir in the tinned tomatoes, beans, stock, sugar, salt and pepper. Turn the heat down to low and pop the lid on tightly. Cook on a low simmer for 1½ hours, gently stirring every now and then. If the gumbo becomes a bit dry, you could add a little water halfway through the cooking.

Stir in the fresh herbs, then check the seasoning and adjust as needed. Leave to cool completely.

TIP: This recipe makes about 2.5 kg (5 lb 8 oz) gumbo, great for feeding a crowd. I like to make a big batch and freeze some in airtight containers for convenience later on. Don't be daunted by the long list of aromatics in the gumbo — the recipe is actually very simple, and totally worth it. For a simple brekkie, you could leave out the tortillas and avocado mash and just serve the warm gumbo with an egg pan-fried in clarified butter oozing over the top. Absolutely delicious.

FOR THE TORTILLAS

Preheat the oven to 180°C (350°F). Line a baking dish with baking paper.

Lay the tortillas on your workbench. Along the centre of each one, add 2 heaped tablespoons (100 g/3½ oz) bean gumbo. Top with the cheese, mint and coriander. Roll each tortilla up tightly into a roll and place on the baking tray, seam side down.

Bake for 15 minutes, or until the tortillas are nice and crispy, and the gumbo and cheese are hot and oozing.

Meanwhile, heat the ghee in a large frying pan, then crack the eggs in and fry for 2 minutes, or until cooked to your liking.

Cut the avocado in half using a sharp knife. Remove the stone, then scoop the flesh into a small bowl. Add the juice of 1 lime, season with a little sea salt and freshly ground black pepper and mash together. Cut the other lime into wedges for serving.

To serve, place a couple of rocket leaves in the centre of six warm plates. Top each with a tortilla and a fried egg. Add a dollop of the avocado mash, sour cream and chilli jam. Serve with the lime wedges for squeezing over.

TORTILLAS

6 flour tortillas, about 25 cm (10 inches) in diameter

¼ quantity Bean gumbo, about 600 g (1 lb 5 oz); see opposite

200 g (7 oz/2 cups) grated cheddar cheese

4 tablespoons roughly chopped mint

1 handful roughly chopped coriander (cilantro)

2 tablespoons ghee (clarified butter)

6 large free-range eggs

1 avocado

2 limes

1 bunch (150 g/5½ oz) rocket (arugula), any tough stems discarded

125 g (4½ oz/½ cup) sour cream

Chilli jam (Toolbox, page 20), for dolloping

No matter how much batter we make, we always run out of corn fritters. And no wonder: this gluten-free brekkie combo is a winner. We also serve baby fritters at cocktail parties, with a spoonful of avocado mash and a crisp shard of grilled prosciutto.

CORN FRITTERS WITH CRISPY BACON, RED CAPSICUM JAM & SOUR CREAM

MAKES **12 FRITTERS**; SERVES **6**
PREPARATION **15 MINUTES + 30 MINUTES RESTING**   COOKING **20 MINUTES**

FRITTERS
270 g (9½ oz) gluten-free plain
   (all-purpose) flour
160 g (5½ oz) gluten-free maize flour
2 tablespoons baking powder
1 tablespoon ground cumin
1 teaspoon ground turmeric
¼ teaspoon chilli powder
2 teaspoons sea salt
4 free-range eggs
400 ml (14 fl oz) milk
500 g (1 lb 2 oz/2½ cups) corn kernels
400 g (14 oz) tin creamed corn
½ bunch (75 g/2½ oz) flat-leaf (Italian)
   parsley, leaves roughly chopped
½ bunch (45 g/1½ oz) coriander
   (cilantro), leaves and stalks roughly
   chopped
1 red capsicum (pepper), diced
1 red onion, diced

TO SERVE
olive oil, for pan-frying
6 bacon rashers
1 bunch (150 g/5½ oz) rocket (arugula),
   any tough stems discarded
200 g (7 oz) sour cream
100 g (3½ oz) Red capsicum jam
   (Toolbox, page 25)
lime weges

To make the fritter batter, sift the flour, maize flour and baking powder into a large bowl. Add the spices and salt, then make a well in the centre. Mix in the eggs one at a time, alternating with the milk, bringing the sides of the mixture in slowly until the batter is smooth.

Add the remaining fritter ingredients and stir to combine. Cover the batter and set aside to rest for 30 minutes.

Preheat the oven to 180°C (350°F). Line a large baking tray with baking paper.

To cook the fritters, place a heavy-based frying pan over medium heat. Pour in a generous amount of oil, to a depth of about 3 cm (1¼ inches), and wait until the oil is nice and hot.

Ladle a good amount of the corn fritter mixture into the oil, to make four fritters, about 8 cm (3¼ inches) in diameter. Cook for 1 minute. Carefully flip the fritters over and cook on the other side. Be careful, because the corn sometimes pops and spits out of the pan. Also, you may need to adjust the heat if your fritters are colouring too quickly on the outside; you don't need to cook the batter all the way through, as we'll be finishing them off in the oven. When you have nice colour on both sides, drain on paper towel, and repeat to make 12 fritters.

Now place all the fritters on the baking tray, then bake for 10 minutes to cook through. Meanwhile, in a clean frying pan, cook the bacon until crispy. Drain on paper towel and keep warm.

Serve the fritters with the rocket, crispy bacon, sour cream and red capsicum jam, with lime wedges on the side.

I love the crunchiness of this — I think it has something to do with the peanut butter and honey. When it first comes out of the oven in heavenly little clusters of joydom, we all stand around the baker's rack, chatting and having a good old go at the super-crunchy bits. It's become a bit of a ritual in our camp.

HOUSE-BAKED BREAKFAST CRUNCH WITH PEANUT BUTTER & HONEY

MAKES **2.5 KG (5 LB 8 OZ)**
PREPARATION **30 MINUTES**   BAKING **15 MINUTES**

450 g (1 lb) runny honey
300 g (10½ oz) crunchy peanut butter
750 g (1 lb 10 oz) rolled (porridge) oats
50 g (1¾ oz) dried apricots, chopped
45 g (1½ oz/¼ cup) sultanas (golden raisins)
300 g (10½ oz) toasted flaked coconut
300 g (10½ oz/2 cups) toasted macadamia nuts, chopped
250 g (9 oz/1⅔ cups) toasted pistachio nuts
55 g (2 oz/⅓ cup) pepitas (pumpkin seeds)

Preheat the oven to 170°C (325°F). Line two large baking trays with baking paper.

In a large saucepan, gently warm the honey and peanut butter until melted, stirring to combine.

Place the oats in a large bowl, pour the melted honey and peanut butter over and mix through. Evenly distribute the mixture over the two baking trays, spreading it out evenly. Don't overcrowd the trays; it's better to cook it in batches if need be.

Bake for 12–16 minutes, or until the mixture is golden. It will get crunchier as it cools, so be patient. Once cooled, place in a large bowl and mix the remaining ingredients through.

Keep in an airtight container in the pantry for breakfasts and midnight snacking.

Chapter Three

PICNIC LUNCHES

ISN'T IT FUNNY HOW FOOD SEEMS TO TASTE SO MUCH BETTER IN THE GREAT OUTDOORS?

And isn't it a lovely way to get people talking — all sprawled out on picnic blankets, sharing their particular plate, and possibly a story behind the recipe on that plate?

The Australian climate is quite conducive to being outdoors most of the year, so as kids we picnicked with our mum and dad and their friends just about every weekend. Now I'm all grown up and with my business hat on, I love creating beautiful picnic food for other people. These are my favourites.

RUSTIC FARMHOUSE PÂTÉ WITH BLOOD ORANGE MARMALADE

MAKES **4 X 450 G (16 OZ) JARS OF PÂTÉ;** RECIPE CAN BE HALVED
PREPARATION **30 MINUTES**　COOKING **30 MINUTES**

CLARIFIED BUTTER
250 g (9 oz) salted butter

PÂTÉ
2 tablespoons olive oil
2 brown onions (about 300 g/10½ oz),
　roughly chopped
2 garlic cloves, crushed
2 thyme sprigs, leaves picked, plus
　extra sprigs for topping the pâté
5 fresh bay leaves, plus extra to garnish
250 g (9 oz) speck or smoked bacon,
　roughly chopped
1 kg (2 lb 4 oz) free-range chicken livers,
　trimmed of any sinew
250 g (9 oz) butter
100 ml (3½ fl oz) brandy
1 teaspoon sea salt
2 tablespoons green peppercorns

TO SERVE
crusty sourdough baguette
Blood orange marmalade (Toolbox,
　page 43)

To prepare the clarified butter, place the butter in a small saucepan and simmer for about 30 minutes, or until all the solids (the milk fats) rise to the top. Skim off and discard these solids. You know the butter is fully clarified when it loses its cloudiness and becomes clear. You'll then be left with the pure golden butter fat, which will be great for preserving your pâté, as it will stop the surface oxidising when you pour it over the top. If not using immediately, your clarified butter will keep in an airtight container in the fridge for up to 1 year.

Meanwhile, to make the pâté, heat the olive oil in a large heavy-based frying pan over medium heat. Sauté the onion, garlic, thyme leaves, bay leaves and speck for 5 minutes, until the onion is transparent.

Add the chicken livers and butter and cook gently for 15–20 minutes, until the livers are cooked through. Remove the bay leaves, then stir in the brandy and salt.

Transfer the mixture to a food processor and blend until smooth. Add the green peppercorns, adjust the seasoning, then spoon into four sterilised jars.

Top each jar of pâté with a bay leaf and an extra thyme sprig or two, then cover with the clarified butter. Seal and store in the refrigerator, where the pâté will keep for several weeks.

For your picnic, take a jar of pâté in a cooler bag, and enjoy with a crusty baguette and your blood orange marmalade.

VIETNAMESE FRESH SPRING ROLLS WITH PRAWN, NASTURTIUM & MINT

MAKES **24**
PREPARATION **40 MINUTES**

24 round rice paper sheets, 25 cm (10 inches) in diameter
24 mint leaves
24 unsprayed nasturtium petals, or petals from other edible flowers
24 cooked prawns (shrimp), peeled
Thai dressing (Toolbox, page 21), to serve
lime wedges, to serve

FILLING
225 g (8 oz) rice vermicelli noodles
1 large carrot, grated
100 g (3½ oz) firm tofu, grated
1 bunch (90 g/3¼ oz) coriander (cilantro), leaves and stalks finely chopped
1 bunch (80 g/2¾ oz) mint, leaves picked and finely chopped
6 spring onions (scallions), finely chopped
50 g (1¾ oz/⅓ cup) peanuts, toasted and chopped
50 g (1¾ oz) fried shallots (from Asian stores)
25 ml (¾ fl oz) Thai dressing (Toolbox, page 21)
sea salt and freshly ground black pepper

Start by making the filling. Put the noodles in a saucepan, cover with cold water and bring to a simmer. Cook for 5 minutes, then drain into a colander. Run cold water over the noodles to stop them cooking any further. Drain well, then leave in the colander on your workbench to dry out.

When the noodles are dry, combine all the other filling ingredients in a large bowl. Season with sea salt and freshly ground black pepper.

To assemble the rolls, have a large bowl of hot water ready, and make sure your workbench is clean and dry. Soak the rice paper sheets in the hot water, one at a time, for 30 seconds, or until just soft, and place on your workbench; it's best to work in small manageable amounts, say five sheets at a time.

Place a mint leaf and a nasturtium petal one-quarter of the way down from the top of each rice sheet. Place a prawn below the garnish. Place a couple of tablespoons of the filling in the middle of each rice sheet. Bring the sides in, crossing over by about 1 cm (½ inch), then roll up firmly to enclose the filling.

Repeat with the remaining ingredients. Serve with Thai dressing as a dipping sauce, and lime wedges for squeezing over.

TIP: These rolls are best made just before serving, but can be packed in a container on a clean damp cloth, then wrapped in plastic wrap to stop them drying out. They are best eaten the day they are made.

The first time I tasted smoked trout was on a trip to Lake Jindabyne as a teen, when we visited a keen fisherman who smoked his own fish. He served his smoked trout on little toasts, with a squeeze of lemon and a bit of horseradish cream.

SMOKED TROUT RILLETTES WITH PICKLED RED ONION ON RYE

SERVES **8**
PREPARATION **30 MINUTES + OVERNIGHT PICKLING**

1 loaf rye bread, thinly sliced, to serve
capers, to garnish

PICKLED RED ONION
2 red onions, thinly sliced
1 tablespoon sugar
1 teaspoon sea salt
250 ml (9 fl oz/1 cup) white wine vinegar
1 tablespoon black peppercorns
2 fresh bay leaves
2 star anise
1 garlic clove, crushed

SMOKED TROUT RILLETTES
1 smoked river trout, weighing about
   350 g (12 oz)
4 spring onions (scallions), finely
   chopped
2 tablespoons finely chopped flat-leaf
   (Italian) parsley
1 tablespoon chopped dill
125 g (4½ oz/½ cup) sour cream
125 g (4½ oz/½ cup) Mayonnaise
   (Toolbox, page 13)
zest of 1 lemon

To prepare the pickled onion, place the onion slices in a colander in the sink and pour boiling water over them. Combine the remaining ingredients in a small glass bowl, stirring to dissolve the sugar and salt. Add the onion, then cover and refrigerate overnight. The pickled onion will be ready to eat the next day, and is at its best during the following week, but will last for a few weeks in the fridge.

For the rillettes, remove and discard the skin from the trout. Flake the flesh away from the bones, taking care to remove all the really fine bones, as they can be hard to see. Place the trout flesh in a bowl, along with the remaining ingredients. Mix with a fork until combined, then season to taste with sea salt and freshly ground black pepper. Cover and keep in the fridge until required; it will keep for up to 7 days.

Serve the rillettes on thin slices of rye bread, topped with the pickled red onion and capers.

This is a great recipe, as the buttermilk tenderises the chicken so it melts in the mouth, while the herbs and garlic added to the crumb make it extra tasty. We love using lots of herbs in our kitchen, so we've added mint and coriander to the slaw, and some of my Thai dressing too. We often pop these chicken drummies in our corporate picnic boxes, or serve them on platters as part of a shared table buffet for country picnics. They go down a treat.

SOUTHERN FRIED CHICKEN WITH CRUNCHY ASIAN SLAW

SERVES **6**
PREPARATION **30 MINUTES + 8 HOURS/OVERNIGHT MARINATING**
COOKING **45 MINUTES**

SOUTHERN FRIED CHICKEN

500 ml (17 fl oz/2 cups) buttermilk

1 large free-range egg

12 free-range chicken drumsticks

300 g (10½ oz/2 cups) plain
   (all-purpose) flour

2 tablespoons finely chopped flat-leaf
   (Italian) parsley

3 thyme sprigs, leaves picked and
   finely chopped

2 garlic cloves, finely chopped

1 tablespoon sea salt

1 teaspoon cayenne pepper

2 teaspoons sweet paprika

2 teaspoons ground cumin

vegetable oil, for pan-frying

FOR THE FRIED CHICKEN

In a large bowl, whisk together the buttermilk and egg. Add the chicken drumsticks, turning to coat all over. Cover and refrigerate for 8 hours or overnight, turning the drumsticks occasionally.

The next day, when ready to cook, preheat the oven to 180°C (350°F). Line a large baking tray with baking paper.

Place the flour, parsley, thyme, garlic, salt and spices in a high-sided tray and mix together.

Shake the excess buttermilk off the drumsticks. Add the drained chicken to the flour mixture and get a good solid coating on each piece. Shake off the excess flour and lay the drumsticks on the baking tray.

Place a heavy-based frying pan over medium–high heat. Pour in about 4 cm (1½ inches) of oil and heat to 180°C (350°F), or until a cube of bread dropped into the oil turns golden brown in 15 seconds.

Working in two batches, cook the chicken for about 5 minutes on each side, or until the coating is golden and crisp. Drain on paper towel.

When you've finished frying all the chicken, place the drumsticks on the baking tray and bake for 25 minutes, or until cooked through; check by inserting a skewer into the thickest part of the drumstick — the juices should run clear.

Allow to cool, then pack into an airtight picnic container and refrigerate until required. Serve sprinkled with sea salt and freshly ground black pepper, with crunchy slaw on the side.

FOR THE SLAW

In a large bowl, toss together the vegetables, chilli and herbs; transfer to an airtight picnic container and refrigerate until required. Just before serving, toss the noodles through the slaw. Mix together the Thai dressing and mayonnaise and drizzle over the slaw at the last minute, to ensure the salad ingredients and noodles stay lovely and crisp.

CRUNCHY SLAW

½ small white cabbage, thinly sliced

1 large carrot, shredded

3 spring onions (scallions), thinly sliced

1 large red chilli, finely chopped

1 bunch (90 g/3¼ oz) coriander (cilantro), leaves and stalks roughly chopped

1 bunch (80 g/2¾ oz) mint, leaves picked and roughly chopped

100 g (3½ oz) packet crunchy fried noodles

125 ml (4 fl oz/½ cup) Thai dressing (Toolbox, page 21)

185 g (6½ oz/¾ cup) Mayonnaise (Toolbox, page 13)

LITTLE LEEK & GRUYÈRE TARTS

MAKES **24**
PREPARATION **40 MINUTES**   COOKING **30 MINUTES**

1 tablespoon olive oil
1 tablespoon butter
2 leeks, pale part only, thinly sliced, washed and dried
2 fresh bay leaves
4 free-range eggs
250 ml (9 fl oz/1 cup) thin (pouring/whipping) cream
1 teaspoon sea salt
¼ teaspoon ground white pepper
1 quantity Shortcrust pastry (Toolbox, page 36)
100 g (3½ oz/1 cup) finely grated gruyère cheese

Preheat the oven to 160°C (315°F). Lightly grease 24 small flan (tart) tins, measuring about 7 cm (2¾ inches) across and 2 cm (¾ inch) deep.

Heat the olive oil and butter in a heavy-based saucepan. Sauté the leek and bay leaves over medium heat for 10 minutes, or until the leek is soft and fragrant. Set aside to cool.

In a bowl, whisk together the eggs, cream, salt and pepper.

On a lightly floured workbench, roll out the pastry to about 3 mm (⅛ inch) thick. Use an 8 cm (3¼ inch) cookie cutter to cut out 24 pastry rounds. Line the tins with the pastry rounds.

Place a heaped teaspoon of the sautéed leek in each, then pour in the egg mixture, about two-thirds of the way up to the top, leaving room for the cheese. Sprinkle with the cheese.

Bake for 15–20 minutes, or until the tarts are a lovely golden colour.

These tarts can be made in advance and stored in an airtight container in the refrigerator for several days, or frozen for a couple of months. Before heading off on your picnic, gently heat them for 10 minutes in a 150°C (300°F) oven to bring them back to room temperature.

FUNKY TOFU, BROWN RICE & AVOCADO NORI ROLLS

MAKES **12 ROLLS, OR 24 PIECES**
PREPARATION **1 HOUR**   COOKING **40 MINUTES**

2 tablespoons chia seeds

225 g (8 oz/1 cup) short-grain brown rice

2 tablespoons sushi vinegar

2 tablespoons toasted sesame seeds

60 g (2¼ oz/¼ cup) Mayonnaise (Toolbox, page 13)

2 teaspoons wasabi paste

12 nori sheets

3 tablespoons pickled ginger, plus extra to serve

1 avocado, cut into 12 wedges

150 g (5½ oz) firm tofu, grated

½ bunch (45 g/1½ oz) coriander (cilantro), leaves picked

small handful of dill sprigs

75 g (2½ oz/1 cup) finely shredded red cabbage

60 ml (2 fl oz/¼ cup) Thai dressing (Toolbox, page 21)

PICKLED CARROT

60 ml (2 fl oz/¼ cup) white wine vinegar

2 tablespoons caster (superfine) sugar

1 teaspoon sea salt

2 carrots, cut into thin batons

Add the chia seeds to the brown rice and cook according to the instructions on the packet; I always use a rice cooker.

Meanwhile, prepare the pickled carrot. In a small saucepan, combine the vinegar, sugar and salt. Stir over high heat until the sugar has dissolved, then add the carrot and cook for 2 minutes. Remove from the heat and leave the carrot to cool in the pickling syrup.

Once the rice is cooked, spread it out on a flat tray, then drizzle the sushi vinegar over. Toss the rice with one hand and fan it with the other, cooling the rice as quickly as possible. Once it has cooled down, add the sesame seeds and toss to combine.

In a small bowl, mix together the mayonnaise and wasabi.

Lay a sushi mat on your workbench. Lay a nori sheet on top, rough side upwards. Place a few heaped tablespoons of the brown rice mixture on the bottom third of the nori sheet. Using wet hands, spread the rice over the nori sheet, leaving about 2.5 cm (1 inch) clear at the top end.

Drizzle a few teaspoons of wasabi mayonnaise along the middle of the rice. Lay some pickled ginger, pickled carrot, an avocado wedge, some tofu, coriander, dill and cabbage all along the middle of the rice, for the length of the nori. Moisten the top edge of the nori with a little water, then roll up tightly. Let the nori rest for a minute or so, before cutting each roll into two. Repeat with the remaining ingredients.

Serve with the Thai dressing for dipping into, and extra pickled ginger.

CORNISH PASTIES

MAKES **ABOUT 20**
PREPARATION **40 MINUTES**   COOKING **40 MINUTES**

2 tablespoons olive oil
1 brown onion, diced
1 carrot, finely diced
2 fresh bay leaves
1 tablespoon tomato paste (concentrated purée)
250 g (9 oz) minced (ground) beef
1 tablespoon cornflour (cornstarch)
1 tablespoon worcestershire sauce
2 teaspoons sea salt
¼ teaspoon ground white pepper
4 tablespoons chopped flat-leaf (Italian) parsley
500 g (1 lb 2 oz) potatoes, peeled, cut into 1 cm (½ inch) dice, then cooked until tender
1 quantity Easy rough puff pastry (Toolbox, page 35)
1 free-range egg, beaten with 60 ml (2 fl oz/¼ cup) milk
Tomato relish (Toolbox, page 14), to serve

Preheat the oven to 180°C (350°F). Line two large baking trays with baking paper.

Heat the olive oil in a large heavy-based saucepan. Add the onion, carrot and bay leaves and sauté over medium heat for 10 minutes, or until the onion and carrot have softened and smell fragrant. Stir in the tomato paste and cook for 3 minutes. Add the beef, breaking it up with a wooden spoon, and cook for 10 minutes, or until the beef is browned and cooked through.

Mix the cornflour with 125 ml (4 fl oz/½ cup) water to make a lump-free slurry, then add to the beef. Stir in the worcestershire sauce, salt, pepper, half the parsley and all the potato, then set aside to cool.

On a lightly floured workbench, roll out the pastry to 5 mm (¼ inch) thick. Use a 14 cm (5½ inch) pastry cutter to cut out 20 pastry rounds. Gather up the remaining pastry and refrigerate or freeze for later use.

Place a couple of heaped tablespoons (about 50 g/1¾ oz) of the beef mixture in the middle of each round. Brush the egg wash around the outside edge of the pastry. Fold the pastry over the mixture, to make a pillow shape, then press the pastry edges together with a fork.

Brush the pasties with more egg yolk and sprinkle with the remaining parsley. Place on the baking trays and bake for 12–15 minutes, or until the pastry is lovely and golden. Serve warm or cold, with a dollop of tomato relish.

TIP: These pasties are best eaten the day they are made. If you'd like to prepare them ahead, you can freeze the unbaked pasties; thaw them in the fridge for 24 hours, then glaze and bake as instructed.

Chapter Four

SUNDAY ROAST

I LOVE BEING INVITED TO PEOPLE'S HOMES FOR LUNCH OR DINNER, BUT IT DOESN'T HAPPEN QUITE AS OFTEN AS I'D LIKE.

I think perhaps people feel they need to perform culinary acrobatics and lay on a spread fit for a queen. If they only knew it is the food in this chapter that I feel most comfortable cooking and serving to my own guests. I am at my happiest throwing a roast with all the trimmings in the oven, closing the oven door and then kicking back for a while.

This is how I cook — relaxed and happy.

> *Meltingly tender and ever so flavoursome, slow-cooked lamb shoulder is my favourite. Don't let the long baking time put you off. The beauty of this dish is that you can do most of the roasting a day or two beforehand if you like, then finish it off in the oven just before your guests arrive — it works brilliantly. You can also turn any leftover lamb, vegies and cooking liquid into a lovely soup by adding pearl barley and more stock.*

SIX-HOUR SLOW-ROASTED LAMB SHOULDER WITH ROSEMARY JUS

SERVES **4**
PREPARATION **40 MINUTES + OVERNIGHT MARINATING**   COOKING **6 HOURS**

1 large carrot, roughly chopped
3 celery stalks, roughly chopped
2 brown onions, roughly chopped
1 garlic bulb, cut in half horizontally
5 fresh bay leaves
3 thyme sprigs
2 rosemary sprigs
1 tablespoon black peppercorns
2 tablespoons balsamic vinegar
1 tablespoon sugar
1 lamb shoulder, about 1.6 kg (3 lb 8 oz),
   on the bone
500 ml (17 fl oz/2 cups) red wine
2 teaspoons sea salt
1 litre (35 fl oz/4 cups) chicken stock
250 ml (9 fl oz/1 cup) Veal jus (Toolbox,
   page 31), optional
½ quantity Mint pesto (Toolbox, page 22)

CHARRED CAPSICUMS
2 red capsicums (peppers)
4 tablespoons olive oil
1 garlic clove, sliced
1 rosemary sprig, leaves picked

Place the chopped vegetables in a large baking dish. Add the garlic, herbs, peppercorns, vinegar and sugar and mix together. Rest the lamb on top. Pour the wine over the lamb, then season it with the salt. Cover and marinate in the fridge overnight, turning it after a few hours.

The next day, preheat the oven to 140°C (275°F). Pour the stock into the dish and turn the lamb again. Cover the lamb with baking paper, then a tight layer of foil. Place in the oven and cook for 5½ hours.

Remove the lamb from the oven. Turn the oven up to 200°C (400°F). Remove the foil and baking paper, then bake the lamb, skin side up, for a further 30 minutes.

Meanwhile, preheat the grill (broiler) to high. Line a baking tray with foil, add the whole capsicums and grill, turning now and then, for about 15 minutes, until the skins have blackened and blistered. Place the capsicums in a plastic bag and leave to sweat for 10 minutes. Slip the skins off the flesh and remove the seeds. Place the capsicum flesh in a bowl with the olive oil, garlic and rosemary and gently mix together.

When the lamb is done, remove it from the oven. Strain 1 litre (35 fl oz/ 4 cups) of the cooking juices from the baking dish, into a clean saucepan. Skim off the oil from the top, place over high heat and cook for about 20 minutes, or until the liquid has reduced by two-thirds and you have a lovely gravy. Stir in the veal jus, if using.

Pull the shoulder blade from the bone; it should just slip out. Serve the lamb with the capsicum and mint pesto, with the gravy on the side.

The idea to stuff a roasted chicken with a sexy, fruity, nutty couscous came when we were thinking about Moroccan influences one day in one of my stores. If you can't fit all the stuffing into the bird, roast the rest of it separately in a buttered shallow baking dish until it gets all golden and crunchy, and serve it alongside. Sometimes I also bake potato wedges in the roasting dish as well, to soak up all those delicious pan juices.

ROASTED CHICKEN WITH COUSCOUS, LEMON & CURRANT STUFFING

SERVES **6**
PREPARATION **30 MINUTES**   COOKING **1 HOUR + 15 MINUTES RESTING**

1.6 kg (3 lb 8 oz) whole free-range chicken, at room temperature
50 g (1¾ oz) cold butter, cut in half
zest and juice of 1 lemon
2 tablespoons olive oil
250 ml (9 fl oz/1 cup) chicken stock

FOR THE STUFFING
250 ml (9 fl oz/1 cup) chicken stock
250 g (9 oz/1⅓ cups) instant couscous
2 tablespoons olive oil
1 red onion, chopped
1 garlic clove, chopped
1 free-range egg, lightly beaten
2 tablespoons chopped coriander (cilantro)
2 tablespoons chopped mint
40 g (1½ oz/¼ cup) toasted pine nuts
40 g (1½ oz/¼ cup) chopped currants
1 teaspoon ground cumin
¼ teaspoon ground allspice
½ teaspoon sea salt
zest and juice of 1 lemon
¼ Preserved lemon (Toolbox, page 27), pith removed, rind chopped

Preheat the oven to 200°C (400°F). Line a baking dish with baking paper.

To prepare the stuffing, heat the chicken stock in a saucepan until hot. Place the couscous in a bowl, pour the hot stock over, then cover with a tea towel and leave to steam for a minute or two. Fluff the couscous grains with a fork.

Place a frying pan on the stove over medium heat. Add the olive oil, then fry the onion and garlic for 10 minutes, or until fragrant. Add the onion mixture to the couscous, along with the rest of the stuffing ingredients. Mix well.

Stuff as much couscous as you can into the chicken cavity. Using kitchen string, tie the legs and parson's nose together. Pull the wings out away from the body, so they'll become seasoned and crispy in the pan. Now gently lift the skin from the breast by carefully prying your fingers under the skin. Slide a piece of butter onto each breast, under the skin. Place the bird in the baking dish. Season well with sea salt and freshly ground black pepper. Sprinkle the lemon zest and juice over, then add the leftover lemon pieces to the baking dish. Drizzle the bird with the olive oil, then pour the stock into the baking dish.

Roast for 30 minutes, then baste the bird with the pan juices. Roast for a final 15 minutes, then remove from the oven. Cover with baking paper and a tea towel and leave to rest for at least 15 minutes.

Serve the bird on a platter, drizzled with the lemony pan juices.

Whenever I come across a fresh, glistening, clear-eyed snapper, this is the dish that springs to mind. Instead of one large snapper, you can cook a plate-sized fish for each person; just reduce the cooking time so they stay moist. This recipe is great as part of a spread or Chinese banquet, or for four people with rice and a big bowl of steamed Chinese vegies. The butter may seem a strange addition, but somehow it just works.

WHOLE ROASTED SNAPPER WITH GINGER, SPRING ONION & SOY

SERVES 4
PREPARATION 20 MINUTES   COOKING 30 MINUTES

2 kg (4 lb 8 oz) snapper, or four 500 g
   (1 lb 2 oz) fish, cleaned and scaled
1 brown onion, sliced
6 spring onions (scallions), roughly
   chopped
2 garlic cloves, chopped
1 thumb-sized piece of fresh ginger,
   thinly sliced
juice of 2 lemons
4 tablespoons soy sauce
100 g (3½ oz) butter, chopped
250 ml (9 fl oz/1 cup) white wine
2 tablespoons peanut oil
Chilli jam (Toolbox, page 20), to serve
coriander (cilantro), to garnish

Preheat the oven to 180°C (350°F). Find a baking dish large enough to fit your fish, then line it with baking paper.

Place the fish on your workbench and check that all the scales have been properly removed. Pat the fish dry, inside and out, with paper towel. Using a sharp knife, score the fish with about six slashes on each side, about 2 cm (¾ inch) deep.

Arrange half the onion, spring onion, garlic and ginger in the baking dish; place the fish on top. Stuff the remaining onion, spring onion, garlic and ginger into the cavity of the fish. Drizzle half the lemon juice and half the soy sauce inside the cavity, along with some leftover lemon bits, then dot with half the butter. Close the fish back up, drizzle with the remaining lemon juice and soy sauce, and dot with the remaining butter. Season the fish with sea salt and freshly ground black pepper.

Pour the wine into the baking dish. Place a sheet of baking paper on top of the fish, cover the whole dish with a piece of foil, then bake for 20 minutes. (If using four small snapper, bake them for 15 minutes.)

Take the fish out of the oven, then remove the foil and baking paper. Turn the oven up to 200°C (400°F). Drizzle the peanut oil over the fish and bake for a further 10 minutes. This should caramelise the fish and increase the stickiness of the sauce a little. Check the fish is cooked by gently inserting a knife into the thickest point, up near the head; the flesh should be opaque.

Serve garnished with coriander, with the pan juices and chilli jam.

> *This is such a fabulous dish when you're entertaining and you need plenty of 'wow' factor without the fuss. If you follow the cooking time perfectly, the beef will be sensational. The red wine jus takes a bit of effort, but adds extra magic to the meal; it can be made well in advance and stashed away in the freezer, ready to impress your guests. It will turn you into a culinary genius overnight.*

PERFECT ROASTED BEEF FILLET WITH POTATO GRATIN & RED WINE JUS

SERVES **6**
PREPARATION **30 MINUTES**   COOKING **1½ HOURS + 20 MINUTES RESTING**

RED WINE JUS

1 tablespoon olive oil
2 French shallots, roughly chopped
2 thyme sprigs
400 ml (14 fl oz) Shiraz
100 ml (3½ fl oz) port
1 litre (35 fl oz/4 cups) beef stock
50 ml (1¾ fl oz) Veal jus (Toolbox, page 31)

TO MAKE THE RED WINE JUS

Heat the olive oil in a heavy-based saucepan. Add the shallot and thyme sprigs and cook over medium heat for 10 minutes, or until the shallot has softened. Add the wine and port and simmer for 20 minutes, or until reduced by half.

Add the stock and simmer again for 20 minutes, to reduce by half.

Strain the liquid into a clean saucepan. Stir in the veal jus and season with sea salt and freshly ground black pepper. The jus should be thick enough to coat the back of a spoon, so if it doesn't, just reduce it a little more to get the desired consistency.

Refrigerate or freeze in airtight containers until required, then just gently heat it just before serving.

NOTE: If you don't have any veal jus handy, you can leave it out and simply whisk a few knobs of chilled butter into the sauce at the end.

FOR THE POTATO GRATIN

Preheat the oven to 160°C (315°F). Butter a shallow casserole dish, measuring about 28 cm x 20 cm (11¼ inches x 8 inches).

Peel the potatoes, then slice as thinly as you can, either in a food processor, or using a mandoline. (If using a mandoline, be very careful as it can catch your fingers.)

In a heavy-based saucepan, bring the cream, garlic, thyme and nutmeg to a simmer over medium heat. Add the potato slices, season with sea salt and freshly ground black pepper and simmer for 10 minutes, gently stirring every now and then. At this point you are just starting the cooking process, so the potato slices will still be a little firm.

Transfer the whole mixture to the casserole. Cover with foil and bake for 40 minutes. Remove the foil, sprinkle the cheese over the top and bake for a further 15 minutes. Keep warm while cooking the beef.

FOR THE BEEF

Preheat the oven to 220°C (425°F). Line a large baking dish with baking paper. Season the beef very liberally with sea salt and freshly ground black pepper, to add flavour and a tasty crust.

Place a heavy-based frying pan over high heat. Once the pan is hot, add the olive oil. Add the beef and leave to caramelise well, turning when each side has plenty of colour, but don't fiddle or move the beef too much. This should take about 10 minutes.

Place the beef in the baking dish. Bake for 12 minutes for rare; please don't be tempted to cook it any longer — I promise it will work. Remove the beef from the oven. Cover with baking paper, then a sheet of foil, and leave to rest for 20 minutes before carving.

Serve with the potato gratin, with the red wine jus on the side. Delicious with crisp steamed green beans.

POTATO GRATIN

butter, for greasing
1 kg (2 lb 4 oz) waxy potatoes, such as bintje (an old Dutch variety with a yellow flesh)
600 ml (21 fl oz) thin (pouring/whipping) cream
1 garlic clove, crushed
2 thyme sprigs
1 teaspoon freshly grated nutmeg
50 g (1¾ oz/½ cup) grated gruyère cheese

FOR THE BEEF

1.2 kg (2 lb 10 oz) fillet of beef
1 tablespoon olive oil

ROASTED PORK BELLY WITH GINGER & SPRING ONION DIPPING SAUCE

SERVES **4**
PREPARATION **30 MINUTES + SEVERAL HOURS DRYING**
COOKING **1½ HOURS + 20 MINUTES RESTING**

1 kg (2 lb 4 oz) organic free-range pork belly
½ teaspoon Chinese five spice
6 spring onions (scallions), roots trimmed
1 thumb-sized piece of fresh ginger, sliced
2 garlic cloves, roughly chopped
1 tablespoon sesame oil
400 g (14 oz/2 cups) long-grain white rice

GINGER & SPRING ONION DIPPING SAUCE
2 thumb-sized pieces of fresh ginger, peeled and grated
4 spring onions (scallions), very finely chopped
1 teaspoon sea salt
185 ml (6 fl oz/¾ cup) peanut oil

Set a wire rack over the sink. Place the pork on the rack, skin side up. Pour boiling water over the top, then pat dry with paper towel.

Line a baking dish with baking paper. Rub the flesh side of the pork belly with the five spice and plenty of sea salt and freshly ground black pepper. Scatter the spring onion, ginger and garlic around the baking dish; place the pork on top, flesh side down. Using a sharp knife, pierce the pork skin all over. Place the baking dish in the fridge, and leave the pork uncovered for a few hours, or overnight if you can afford the time.

When you're ready to cook, preheat the oven to 160°C (315°F). Rub the pork with the sesame oil and sprinkle liberally with more sea salt. Bake the pork for 1½ hours. After this time, if the skin hasn't quite crackled up enough, turn the oven up to 180°C (350°F) with the grill element on, and blast the pork for 15–30 minutes, or until the crackling is super crisp and golden. Remove from the oven and rest for 20 minutes.

Meanwhile, cook the rice following the packet instructions, or your rice cooker instructions. (I always rinse the rice twice before cooking it, then cover with enough cold water so it just covers my hand when I lay my palm flat on the top of the rice. It always turns out perfectly!)

To make the dipping sauce, combine the ginger, spring onion and salt in a small heatproof bowl. In a small saucepan, heat the peanut oil until smoking, then very carefully pour the oil over the ginger and spring onion. Mix with a spoon to combine, then set aside for serving; the dipping sauce can be made a day or two ahead if needed.

Cut the pork into pieces. Serve with the dipping sauce and rice.

This is a recipe from my sister, Joey, who is a great cook and my harshest culinary critic. When I go to her place for dinner, this is one of the dishes I always request. She serves it with baby potatoes and a crisp rocket salad from her garden. We all get stuck in with our fingers, enjoying a sticky, salty, lemony good time.

ROASTED SPATCHCOCKS WITH GREEN OLIVES, FENNEL & LEMON

SERVES **4**
PREPARATION **15 MINUTES**   COOKING **20 MINUTES + 10 MINUTES RESTING**

2 large spatchcocks
2 fennel bulbs, sliced, leaving the
  fronds attached if you wish
100 g (3½ oz) green olives
250 g (9 oz) cherry tomatoes
3 garlic cloves, roughly chopped
1 large red chilli, roughly chopped
1 Preserved lemon (Toolbox, page 27),
  pith cut out, rind thinly sliced
1 tablespoon dried oregano
2 teaspoons sea salt
125 ml (4 fl oz/½ cup) white wine
juice of 1 lemon
2 tablespoons olive oil

Preheat the oven to 180°C (350°F). Line a large baking dish with baking paper.

Using chicken shears, cut each spatchcock down each side of the backbone, discarding the bone. Flatten out the birds. Using a sharp knife, cut down the breastbone, so you have two halves. Discard the giblets. Wash the birds under cold water and pat dry with paper towel.

Place the birds in the baking dish, skin side up. Scatter the fennel, olives and tomatoes around the dish. Sprinkle with the garlic, chilli, preserved lemon, oregano and salt, then add a good sprinkling of freshly ground black pepper. Drizzle with the wine, lemon juice and olive oil.

Roast for 20 minutes, or until the birds are gently caramelised, and the juices run clear when tested with a skewer at the thickest point.

Cover with foil and leave to rest for 10 minutes, before serving with the pan juices.

Chapter Five

FRESH &
FRAGRANT SALADS

SALADS PLAY A BIG PART IN MY LIFE, BOTH AT HOME AND AT WORK.

We try to have at least two or three gorgeous salads in our store window each day, as I know we are all trying to be more mindful of what we put into our bodies.

When I think about what a salad needs, I always put my healthy hat on and incorporate lots of grains, pulses and beans. Root vegies play a big part too, and I'm mad about using fresh herbs and dried fruits for extra flavour, and a sprinkling of nuts for texture and crunch.

Here's a selection of my favourite salads, which I've been tossing for the past 20 years.

This is one of the first salads I made to sell in the store. People would come in especially for it, and then have a mini meltdown if it wasn't on the menu that day. It is so lovely and lively with the freshness of the aromatic herbs and piquant pineapple. Roasting the hokkien noodles makes them kind of chewy and crunchy in parts — quite addictive! — while toasted peanuts add a great textural crunch at the end. This quantity is perfect as part of a lunch buffet for at least 10 friends. Instead of chicken, you could use seared beef fillet or barbecued prawns.

POACHED COCONUT CHICKEN SALAD WITH ROASTED HOKKIEN NOODLES

SERVES **10** AS PART OF A SHARED-PLATES TABLE
PREPARATION **30 MINUTES**   COOKING **30 MINUTES**

500 g (1 lb 2 oz) skinless free-range chicken breast fillets

400 ml (14 fl oz) tin coconut milk

1 lemongrass stem

1 bunch (90 g/3¼ oz) coriander (cilantro)

1 thumb-sized piece of fresh ginger, peeled and sliced

3 star anise

500 g (1 lb 2 oz) hokkien (egg) noodles

125 ml (4 fl oz/½ cup) Thai dressing (Toolbox, page 21)

1 bunch (80 g/2¾ oz) mint, leaves picked

1 red capsicum (pepper), thinly sliced

1 large carrot, julienned

2 Lebanese (short) cucumbers, peeled, seeded and sliced on the diagonal

¼ small white cabbage, thinly sliced

250 g (9 oz) cherry tomatoes, cut in half

¼ sweet pineapple, peeled and chopped into chunks

1 large red chilli, chopped

2 tablespoons toasted sesame seeds

100 g (3½ oz/⅔ cup) peanuts, toasted and chopped

Preheat the oven to 180°C (350°F).

Prepare the chicken by placing it in a baking dish and seasoning with sea salt and freshly ground black pepper. Pour the coconut milk over the top, then add enough water to just cover the chicken. Bruise the lemongrass stem with the back of a heavy knife, then add to the baking dish. Take the bunch of coriander, cut off the roots, give them a good wash, then add them to the dish with the ginger and star anise. Roughly chop the coriander stalks and leaves and set aside for later.

Cover the dish with baking paper, then a sheet of foil. Transfer to the oven and bake for 20–30 minutes, or until the chicken is cooked through and tender. Remove from the oven and leave to cool in the stock, then slice or tear the chicken into strips, reserving the stock for another use.

Meanwhile, line a baking tray with baking paper. Cut the noodles in half and spread them on the tray. Drizzle with half the Thai dressing and bake for 10 minutes. Remove from the oven and leave to cool.

Put the noodles and chicken in a large bowl. Add the reserved chopped coriander and the mint, along with the vegetables, cherry tomatoes, pineapple and chilli. Toss together well. Sprinkle with the sesame seeds and peanuts, drizzle with the remaining Thai dressing and serve.

> *Couscous is such a great everyday pantry ingredient. You can steam a few cups of it, add some nuts, dried fruit, fresh herbs, and almost anything from the fridge including leftover vegies from the night before, and there you have an instant meal.*

COUSCOUS, ROASTED VEGETABLE & SWEET CORN SALAD

SERVES **10** AS PART OF A SHARED-PLATES TABLE
PREPARATION **40 MINUTES**   COOKING **30 MINUTES**

380 g (13½ oz/2 cups) instant couscous
1 teaspoon ground turmeric
1 tablespoon ground cumin
440 g (15½ oz) tin chickpeas, rinsed
    and drained
1 bunch (90 g/3¼ oz) coriander (cilantro),
    leaves and stalks roughly chopped
1 bunch (80 g/2¾ oz) mint, chopped
1 bunch (150 g/5½ oz) flat-leaf (Italian)
    parsley, leaves chopped
3 corn cobs, kernels removed
1 red onion, finely diced
250 g (9 oz) cherry tomatoes, cut in half
85 g (3 oz/½ cup) sultanas (golden
    raisins)
40 g (1½ oz/¼ cup) toasted pine nuts
40 g (1½ oz/¼ cup) toasted almonds,
    chopped
zest and juice of 2 lemons
2 tablespoons olive oil
1 quantity Tahini yoghurt dressing
    (Toolbox, page 16)

ROASTED VEGETABLES
500 g (1 lb 2 oz) pumpkin (winter
    squash), diced
1 eggplant (aubergine), diced
1 red capsicum (pepper), diced
1 tablespoon sweet paprika
4 tablespoons olive oil

Start by roasting the vegetables. Preheat the oven to 180°C (350°F). Line a large baking tray with baking paper.

Put the pumpkin, eggplant and capsicum in a large bowl. Sprinkle with the paprika and drizzle with the olive oil. Toss well, spread the vegetables out on the baking tray and season with sea salt and freshly ground black pepper. Roast for 20–30 minutes, or until nice and caramelised, then remove from the oven and leave to cool.

Put the couscous, turmeric and cumin in a bowl. Pour 750 ml (12 fl oz/ 3 cups) boiling water over, cover with plastic wrap and leave to steam for 3 minutes. Rake a fork through to make the couscous nice and fluffy, then cover again for another 5 minutes. Uncover and fork again, breaking down any lumps. Leave to cool.

Tip the couscous into a large mixing bowl, along with the roasted vegies. Add all the remaining ingredients, except the tahini yoghurt dressing. Season to taste with salt and pepper and toss together until well combined.

Serve in a lovely big, bright Moroccan-style dish, with the tahini dressing on the side.

> *Kale is such a gorgeous curly-leafed vegetable, and becomes so ridiculously green when you cook it that you can't help thinking how good it is for you. I really enjoy its chewiness, and the way it holds its shape even after cooking. I also love its versatility — you can fry it, bake it, stir-fry it, add it to soups and curries, and use it in salads such as this.*

KALE, PEA, MINT & FARRO SALAD WITH LEMON DRESSING

SERVES **UP TO 10** AS A SIDE DISH
PREPARATION **15 MINUTES**　COOKING **30 MINUTES**

500 g (1 lb 2 oz) packet farro (see Tip)
4 tablespoons olive oil
2 garlic cloves, chopped
1 bunch kale, stalks removed, leaves
　roughly chopped
juice of 1 lemon
½ teaspoon sea salt
500 g (1 lb 2 oz) packet frozen green
　peas
1 bunch (80 g/2¾ oz) mint, leaves picked
250 g (9 oz) feta cheese

Cook the farro according to the packet instructions until it is just tender, but still has a chewy bite. Set aside to cool.

Heat half the olive oil in a wok or large frying pan over high heat, then fry the garlic for 1–2 minutes, or until fragrant and a bit nutty. Add the kale and cook for 5 minutes, until softened and bright green. Squeeze the lemon juice over the kale and sprinkle with the salt.

Meanwhile, cook the peas in a saucepan of boiling salted water for 3 minutes, then drain and refresh under cold running water.

In a large bowl, combine the farro, kale and peas. Add the mint, drizzle with the remaining olive oil and season with sea salt and freshly ground black pepper. Toss together and place on a platter. Crumble the feta over the top. Serve while the flavours are fresh and perky.

TIP: Similar in appearance to brown rice or barley, farro is an ancient wheat variety with a chewy, nutty texture. Rather than cooking the farro in a pot of boiling water, I cook it in my rice cooker, as this seems to work really well; simply follow your rice cooker instructions for cooking rice.

With so many of us gluten-free these days, it's nice to be able to chow into a dish such as this one, powered with the super flavours of fresh ginger, soy and sesame.

SUPER SOBA NOODLE SALAD

SERVES **10** AS PART OF A SHARED-PLATES TABLE
PREPARATION **30 MINUTES**   COOKING **10 MINUTES**

200 g (7 oz) packet of buckwheat
   (soba) noodles
1 tablespoon sesame oil
200 g (7 oz) button mushrooms, sliced
100 g (3½ oz) firm tofu, grated
¼ white cabbage, thinly sliced
6 spring onions (scallions), thinly sliced
1 thumb-sized piece of fresh ginger,
   peeled and grated
200 g (7 oz) baby English spinach leaves
1 red capsicum (pepper), thinly sliced
50 g (1¾ oz/⅓ cup) toasted sesame seeds
50 g (1¾ oz/¼ cup) pickled ginger,
   chopped
1 bunch (90 g/3¼ oz) coriander (cilantro),
   leaves and stalks chopped
2 tablespoons light soy sauce
1 avocado, sliced
2 nori sheets

FOR THE OMELETTE
2 teaspoons vegetable oil
4 free-range eggs
1 tablespoon soy sauce
1 tablespoon toasted sesame seeds
2 tablespoons chopped coriander

FOR THE DRESSING
½ garlic clove, finely chopped
1 tablespoon miso paste
1 tablespoon light soy sauce
1 tablespoon pickled ginger juice
juice of 1 lemon

Start by making the omelette. Place a large non-stick frying pan over high heat. Add the vegetable oil. In a bowl, whisk the eggs, soy sauce, sesame seeds and coriander until combined. When the oil is hot, pour the egg mixture into the pan and move the pan around so the egg covers the whole base. After 1 minute, gently pull the egg away from the side of the pan, into the middle, and tilt the pan so the uncooked egg moves into the spaces created. Cook for a further 2 minutes, or until the omelette is cooked. Slide it out onto a plate to cool, then roll the omelette up into a log, cut into thin slices and set aside.

Meanwhile, cook the noodles following the packet directions. Drain, then gently toss the sesame oil through the noodles to stop them sticking together.

Mix all the dressing ingredients together, adding a little water to give a nice pouring consistency. Check the seasoning.

Place the noodles in a large bowl. Add all the other salad ingredients, except the avocado and nori. Drizzle the salad with the dressing and toss; this salad is best dressed just before sering time.

Pile the salad onto a large serving platter and top with the avocado and omelette. Lastly, with a pair of scissors, snip the nori sheets into thin strips or funky shapes and scatter them over the salad. Serve straightaway.

I tried this salad at Kepos Street Kitchen, a Middle Eastern and Mediterranean-inspired restaurant in Sydney's inner city, and loved it. The next day I made my own version, shown here — isn't imitation the highest form of flattery?

PEARL BARLEY, ROASTED CAULIFLOWER & CRANBERRY SALAD

SERVES **4**
PREPARATION **30 MINUTES**   COOKING **45 MINUTES**

200 g (7 oz/1 cup) pearl barley
1 small cauliflower, cut into chunky pieces
2 teaspoons ground turmeric
1 tablespoon ground sumac
2 tablespoons olive oil
2 tablespoons roughly chopped dill
4 tablespoons roughly chopped mint
1 bunch (150 g/5½ oz) flat-leaf (Italian)
   parsley, leaves picked and roughly
   chopped
30 g (1 oz/¼ cup) walnuts, toasted
   and chopped
75 g (2½ oz/½ cup) pistachio nuts,
   toasted and chopped
75 g (2½ oz/½ cup) dried cranberries
1 pomegranate, seeded
100 g (3½ oz) creamy feta cheese,
   crumbled

DRESSING
zest and juice of 1 lemon
3 tablespoons pomegranate molasses
3 tablespoons olive oil
¼ garlic clove, crushed

Add the barley to a saucepan and pour in 500 ml (17 fl oz/2 cups) water. Bring to a simmer, then cook over medium heat for 40 minutes, or until the water has been absorbed; the barley should still be a bit nutty. Set aside to cool.

Meanwhile, preheat the oven to 180°C (350°F). Line a baking dish with baking paper. In a bowl, toss together the cauliflower, turmeric, sumac and olive oil. Spread the cauliflower over the baking tray and roast for 15–20 minutes, or until the cauliflower is a little caramelised. Remove from the oven and leave to cool.

Place the cooled barley and cauliflower in a large bowl or serving dish. Add the herbs, nuts and cranberries.

Mix all the dressing ingredients together and season to taste with sea salt. Toss the salad with enough of the dressing to moisten it, but not drown it. At this point you could cover and leave the salad for a few hours if making it in advance; simply rain down those pomegranate seeds and dot with the feta just before serving.

Every family has a favourite potato salad — here is mine. We offer this one on our catering menu as a buffet item. I think the seeded mustard really makes this dish: the grains have the perfect piquancy, they're nice and plump and pop in your mouth.

BABY POTATOES WITH SOUR CREAM & SEEDED MUSTARD DRESSING

SERVES **10** AS PART OF A SHARED-PLATES TABLE
PREPARATION **10 MINUTES** COOKING **15 MINUTES**

1.5 kg (3 lb 5 oz) baby potatoes,
  cut in half
150 g (5½ oz) salted butter
15 fresh sage leaves
125 g (4½ oz/½ cup) sour cream
125 g (4½ oz/½ cup) Mayonnaise
  (Toolbox, page 13)
2 tablespoons seeded mustard
zest and juice of 1 lemon
4 spring onions (scallions), thinly sliced
4 tablespoons chopped flat-leaf (Italian)
  parsley

Place the potatoes in a saucepan and cover with cold water. Bring to the boil over high heat, then reduce the heat to medium and cook for 10–15 minutes, or until just tender. Drain and set aside to cool.

Melt the butter in a frying pan. Add the sage leaves and toss over low heat until the butter is nut brown and the sage is crisp.

In a small bowl, mix together the sour cream, mayonnaise, mustard, lemon zest, lemon juice, spring onion and parsley.

Place the cooled potatoes in a bowl. Add the sour cream dressing, then season to taste with sea salt and freshly ground black pepper. Gently toss to combine.

Drizzle the nut-brown butter over the top, garnish with the crispy sage leaves and serve.

TIP: If making this salad a few hours ahead, fry the sage leaves just before serving and scatter them over the potatoes at the last minute.

> *I'm a late starter when it comes to quinoa, having only discovered it in the past year or so, but now I'm making up for lost time. Quinoa is very high up in the super-food chain, so it's good to get it into you whenever you can. We love this salad!*

HERBY QUINOA & ROASTED VEGETABLE SALAD

SERVES 6–10
PREPARATION 30 MINUTES   COOKING 25 MINUTES

600 g (1 lb 5 oz) pumpkin (winter squash)
2 eggplants (aubergines)
2 red capsicums (peppers)
1 red onion
6 tablespoons olive oil
2 garlic cloves, crushed
1 tablespoon sweet paprika
200 g (7 oz/1 cup) quinoa
4 tablespoons roughly chopped dill
1 bunch (80 g/2¾ oz) mint, leaves picked and roughly chopped
4 tablespoons roughly chopped flat-leaf (Italian) parsley
150 g (5½ oz) baby English spinach leaves
45 g (1½ oz/¼ cup) raisins
40 g (1½ oz/¼ cup) almonds
zest and juice of 2 lemons
1 pomegranate, seeded
200 g (7 oz) Labneh (Toolbox, page 28)

Preheat the oven to 180°C (350°F). Line a large baking tray with baking paper.

Peel the pumpkin and chop into 2 cm (¾ inch) chunks, then cut the eggplants, capsicums and onion the same size. Place in a bowl and drizzle with 4 tablespoons of the olive oil. Add the garlic, paprika and a good sprinkling of sea salt and freshly ground black pepper and toss until well coated.

Tip the vegetables onto the baking tray and bake for 20 minutes, or until they are soft and caramelised. Remove from the oven and leave to cool.

Meanwhile, add the quinoa and 500 ml (17 fl oz/2 cups) water to a saucepan. Bring to the boil, then reduce the heat and simmer for 15–20 minutes, or until the water has been absorbed, stirring every now and then. Set aside to cool.

Put the roasted vegetables in a large mixing bowl. Add the quinoa, herbs, spinach, raisins, almonds, lemon zest, lemon juice and remaining olive oil. Gently toss together, then check the seasoning. At this point you could cover and leave the salad for a few hours if making ahead.

When you're ready to eat, arrange the salad on a platter. Scatter the pomegranate seeds over, top with the labneh and serve.

Quite often I'll whip up this colourful salad for a breezy Sunday lunch. I'll boil some extra eggs at breakfast, and use up those left-over potatoes from the night before. The ingredients can be quite flexible, although I do like to layer them and serve the dressing on the side, so the salad remains pretty and everyone gets a little bit of everything. We make this salad at least once a week in our stores.

FANCY TUNA NIÇOISE WITH LEMON DRESSING

SERVES **4**
PREPARATION **30 MINUTES**

2 baby cos (romaine) lettuces, outer leaves discarded
2 cooked potatoes, skin on
440 g (15½ oz) tin good-quality tuna, drained and flaked into chunks
2 vine-ripened tomatoes, each cut into 8 wedges
½ red onion, thinly sliced
4 boiled eggs, peeled and quartered
12 olives (black, green or a mixture of both)
2 tablespoons baby salted capers, rinsed and drained
8 anchovies, cut in half lengthways
small handful of dill sprigs
1 quantity Lemon, garlic & dijon dressing (Toolbox, page 17)

Tear the leaves off each lettuce and arrange them around a large, shallow salad bowl.

Slice the potatoes and artfully layer them over the lettuce, followed by the tuna, tomato wedges, onion and eggs. Top with the olives, capers, anchovies and dill, placing them strategically for maximum taste and beauty.

By layering the salad, and serving the dressing on the side, it will stay fresh and perky — and if you don't manage to eat all the salad, it will last a day or two in the fridge, covered with plastic wrap.

This salad is super hippie, but I just can't resist the nuttiness of brown rice. The colour and texture of the broccolini and roasted sweet potato work wonderfully with the sharpness of the feta, complementing the rice perfectly. If there's any salad left over, this is a good one to take to work in your lunchbox with a little tin of chilli-flavoured tuna to pile on top — yummy and nutritious.

BROWN RICE SALAD WITH FETA & ROASTED SWEET POTATO

SERVES 4–6
PREPARATION **20 MINUTES**   COOKING **40 MINUTES**

400 g (14 oz/2 cups) long-grain brown rice
300 g (10½ oz) broccolini, stalks trimmed 2.5 cm (1 inch) from the end
1 teaspoon sea salt
1 small red onion, thinly sliced
4 tablespoons roughly chopped coriander (cilantro) stalks and leaves
100 g (3½ oz) creamy feta cheese, crumbled
2 tablespoons fried shallots (from Asian stores)

FOR THE SWEET POTATO
2 kg (4 lb 8 oz) orange sweet potatoes
4 tablespoons olive oil
2 teaspoons ground cumin
1 teaspoon ground cinnamon
½ teaspoon sea salt
¼ teaspoon freshly ground black pepper

FOR THE DRESSING
3 tablespoons olive oil
1 tablespoon honey
2 tablespoons red wine vinegar
1 garlic clove, crushed
½ teaspoon sea salt

Start by roasting the sweet potatoes. Preheat the oven to 180°C (350°F). Line a baking tray or baking dish with baking paper.

Peel the sweet potatoes and cut into wedges. Place in a large bowl, along with the olive oil, cumin, cinnamon, salt and pepper. Toss until well coated, then arrange on the baking tray and bake for 30 minutes, or until the sweet potato is golden and cooked through. Remove from the oven and leave to cool.

Meanwhile, cook the rice according to the packet instructions; drain the rice and leave to cool. If using a rice cooker, add the rice and 1.25 litres (44 fl oz/5 cups) water to the cooker and cook until done.

Three-quarters fill a medium-sized saucepan with water, add the salt and bring to the boil. Add the broccolini and cook for 3 minutes. Drain, then refresh in ice-cold water to keep the broccolini super green.

Combine the dressing ingredients, adding some freshly ground black pepper to taste. Place the cooled sweet potato and rice in a large mixing bowl, along with the broccolini, onion and coriander. Drizzle with the dressing, toss together and adjust the seasoning.

Serve in a big shallow bowl, topped with the feta and fried shallots.

I love how all the various components of this salad bring so many different layers of flavour and texture to the table. The smokiness and silkiness of the trout meets the piquancy of sour mango, the crunch of fried shallots and peanuts, and the salty sweetness of nam jim. This is what Thai food is all about. This gorgeous salad would be lovely on Chinese spoons with the trout on top as a nice little pass-around, or served on a plate dressed with a banana leaf as part of a main meal.

SMOKED TROUT SALAD WITH GREEN MANGO, MINT & NAM JIM

SERVES **6**
PREPARATION **30 MINUTES**

2 smoked river trout, weighing about 200 g (7 oz) each

2 green mangoes, peeled and shredded

3 red Asian shallots, thinly sliced

1 long red chilli, seeded and thinly sliced

1 long green chilli, seeded and thinly sliced

1 bunch (80 g/2¾ oz) mint, leaves picked

1 bunch (90 g/3¼ oz) coriander (cilantro), leaves and stalks roughly chopped

2 tablespoons peanuts, toasted and chopped

2 tablespoons fried shallots (from Asian stores)

100 g (3½ oz) jar of salmon roe

lime cheeks, to serve

1 quantity Nam jim (Toolbox, page 19)

Remove and discard the skin from the trout. Flake the flesh away from the bones, taking care to remove all the really fine bones, as they can be hard to see.

Place the trout flesh in a mixing bowl. Add the mango, sliced shallot, chilli and herbs and gently toss.

Line a plate or platter with a banana leaf. Pile the salad on top, then sprinkle with the peanuts and fried shallot. Top with the salmon roe and serve with lime cheeks and nam jim.

TIP: This salad is so versatile. You can omit the smoked trout and salmon roe, and instead use barbecued duck, rare roast beef, or prawns (shrimp) straight off the barbecue.

Incredibly quick, but with plenty of WOW, this recipe was given to me by a colleague, Kirsten Harris, a dynamo who is the best time manager I know. In summer, you could get a bit fancy and chop some mango, peach or nectarine over the top.

EASY BARBECUED CHICKEN SALAD WITH THAI DRESSING

SERVES **4–6**
PREPARATION **15 MINUTES**

1 barbecued chicken, shredded
200 g (7 oz) baby English spinach leaves
200 g (7 oz) mesclun salad mix
200 g (7 oz) bean sprouts
1 bunch (80 g/2¾ oz) mint, leaves picked
1 bunch (90 g/3¼ oz) coriander
   (cilantro), leaves and stalks roughly
   chopped
250 g (9 oz) cherry tomatoes, cut in half
125 ml (4 fl oz/½ cup) Thai dressing
   (Toolbox, page 21)
roughly chopped toasted peanuts,
   for sprinkling
3 tablespoons fried shallots (from Asian
   stores), optional

In a large mixing bowl, toss together the chicken, spinach, mesclun, bean shoots, herbs and tomatoes. Arrange over a serving platter, or place in a large serving bowl.

Drizzle with the Thai dressing, then sprinkle with the peanuts and the fried shallots, if using. Serve straightaway.

Great as part of a winter-table shared platter, this salad looks really rustic alongside roast lamb. I love the earthiness of the beets and carrots. Don't peel them, as that's half their charm, and there's plenty of goodness in the skins too.

PUY LENTIL SALAD WITH BEETROOT, ROASTED BABY CARROTS & LABNEH

SERVES 6
PREPARATION **30 MINUTES**   COOKING **30 MINUTES**

6–8 baby beetroot (beets)
6–8 baby carrots
4 tablespoons olive oil
1 tablespoon ground sumac
1 garlic glove, crushed
500 g (1 lb 2 oz) puy lentils
1 fresh bay leaf
1 red onion, finely diced
2 vine-ripened tomatoes, diced
1 bunch (80 g/2¾ oz) mint, leaves picked and chopped
1 bunch (150 g/5½ oz) flat-leaf (Italian) parsley, leaves picked and chopped
2 bunches (300 g/10½ oz) rocket (arugula)
150 g (5½ oz) Labneh (Toolbox, page 28)

BALSAMIC DRESSING
4 tablespoons balsamic vinegar
6 tablespoons olive oil
1 tablespoon honey

Preheat the oven to 180°C (350°F). Line a baking tray with baking paper.

Trim the leaves and stalks of the beetroot and carrots, leaving about 10 cm (4 inches) of stalk still attached. Place on the baking tray, drizzle with the olive oil and sprinkle with the sumac and garlic. Season with sea salt and freshly ground black pepper and roast for 20 minutes, or until the vegetables are cooked and caramelised.

Meanwhile, place the lentils, bay leaf and onion in a saucepan. Cover with cold water, then bring to the boil. Reduce the heat to a rapid simmer and cook for about 20 minutes, or until just tender. Drain.

Mix together the balsamic dressing ingredients, adding salt and pepper to taste.

Place the lentil mixture in a mixing bowl. Add the tomatoes, mint and half the parsley, then gently fold through half the balsamic dressing. Leave to marinate for an hour or so.

To serve, arrange the rocket on a large platter, then top with the lentils. Arrange the beetroot, carrots and labneh around. Drizzle with the remaining dressing and sprinkle with the remaining parsley.

Not bad for a salad that was invented 80-odd years ago. The secret to this version is to layer all the ingredients so it looks fresh and modern, and so you get a little bit of everything with every bite. An oldie but a goodie, and our customers love it.

HERBED CHICKEN CAESAR SALAD WITH GARLIC CROÛTES

SERVES **4–6**
PREPARATION **30 MINUTES + 1 HOUR MARINATING**   COOKING **30 MINUTES**

---

800 g (1 lb 12 oz) free-range chicken
  breast fillets, skin on
1 garlic clove, finely chopped
2 teaspoons herbes de Provence
  (a mix of dried herbs)
zest and juice of 1 lemon
2 tablespoons olive oil
200 g (7 oz) bacon rashers, thinly sliced
2 baby cos (romaine) lettuces, cut
  lengthways into wedges
6 free-range eggs, hard-boiled, shelled
  and grated
100 g (3½ oz) parmesan cheese, grated
½ bunch (75 g/2½ oz) flat-leaf (Italian)
  parsley, leaves picked and finely
  chopped

DRESSING
5 anchovy fillets, finely chopped
235 g (8½ oz/1 cup) Mayonnaise
  (Toolbox, page 13)
2 tablespoons worcestershire sauce
zest and juice of 1 lemon
1 garlic clove, crushed

GARLIC CROÛTES
¼ loaf sourdough batard
2 tablespoons olive oil
1 garlic clove, finely chopped

Place the chicken, garlic, herbes de Provence and lemon zest and lemon juice in a bowl. Season with sea salt and freshly ground black pepper, mixing to coat the chicken. Cover and marinate in the fridge for 1 hour.

Meanwhile, place all the dressing ingredients in a bowl. Season to taste with salt and pepper and whisk together, adding a tablespoon or so of water to obtain a good pouring consistency. Set aside.

Preheat the oven to 180°C (350°F). Line a baking tray with baking paper.

To make the garlic croûtes, cut the bread in half horizontally, then cut vertically into thin slices. Place in a bowl. Drizzle with the olive oil, sprinkle with the garlic, season with salt and pepper and toss. Spread the slices on the baking tray and bake for 10–15 minutes, or until the croûtes are golden. Remove from the tray and set aside, leaving the oven on.

In a heavy-based frying pan, heat the olive oil over medium heat. Sear the chicken breasts two at a time for 4 minutes on each side, or until caramelised. Transfer to the baking tray and roast for 10–15 minutes, or until cooked through. Remove from the oven and leave to cool slightly.

In the same frying pan you cooked the chicken in, fry the bacon until golden and crisp. Drain on paper towel and leave to cool.

Lay half the lettuce leaves on a platter. Slice the chicken and arrange half over the lettuce. Scatter with half the egg, then the bacon, then the parmesan. Repeat with the remaining lettuce, chicken, egg, bacon and parmesan. Top with the croûtes and sprinkle the parsley over. Drizzle with some of the dressing, and serve the rest on the side.

Chapter Six

SOUPS, PASTAS, BRAISES & A FEW OTHERS

WHEN COMPILING A LIST OF MY MOST
CHERISHED DISHES FOR THIS CHAPTER,
I WONDERED HOW MANY HOMES THEY
MAY HAVE BEEN SERVED IN DURING
THE PAST 25 YEARS.

It made me feel a bit warm and fuzzy, and this is the reason we call
these dishes 'home meal therapy'. These are the dishes that wind up
on the tables of super-busy people who don't have time to cook, but
still want to nurture themselves — and the people they love — with
homemade beautiful food.

Every morning in our stores, we have a 'culinary pow wow', where
we come together and bounce ideas on what we'll cook for that
evening's meals, driven very much by what is in season and fresh
in the markets. I really enjoy these team meetings. They get my
creative juices going — and because we're all such passionate
foodies, sharing ideas around the table, I'm always learning
something new.

Roasted Jerusalem artichoke has a deep, mellow, almost nutty flavour in this elegant yet heart-warming soup; a little drizzle of truffle oil is the full stop that makes this soup extraordinary. It's great with toasted sourdough, but I also love making a double quantity and serving it in little shot glasses at a winter cocktail party, to warm the guests up and get their palates ready for the fabulous dishes to come.

ROASTED JERUSALEM ARTICHOKE SOUP WITH TRUFFLE OIL

SERVES **8–10 WITH LEFTOVERS**
PREPARATION **30 MINUTES**   COOKING **1 HOUR**

6 garlic cloves, peeled
1½ tablespoons olive oil
ground white pepper, for seasoning
500 g (1 lb 2 oz) Jerusalem artichokes
2 tablespoons butter
2 leeks, pale part only, roughly chopped
4 fresh bay leaves
1 litre (35 fl oz/4 cups) vegetable stock
1 tablespoon truffle oil, plus extra to serve
60 ml (2 fl oz/¼ cup) thin (pouring/ whipping) cream

Preheat the oven to 160°C (315°F).

Place the garlic cloves in a piece of foil, drizzle with 2 teaspoons of the olive oil and sprinkle with sea salt and ground white pepper. Fold up into a well-sealed parcel, then roast for 1 hour, or until the garlic mellows and caramelises. Remove from the oven and set aside.

Gently scrub the Jerusalem artichokes, then thinly slice.

Heat the butter and remaining olive oil in a heavy-based saucepan over medium–high heat. Add the artichoke, leek and bay leaves and cook for 10 minutes, or until the artichoke and leek soften. Stir in the stock, truffle oil and roasted garlic. Cook for a further 20 minutes, then allow to cool slightly.

Using a food processor or hand blender, purée the soup until smooth. Stir in the cream and adjust the seasoning, then gently reheat.

Serve drizzled with a little extra truffle oil.

This is such a colourful dish, and the flavours don't disappoint either. With a bowl of steaming hot rice, it makes a great mid-week dinner, especially with a little Chilli jam (page 20). If you are vegetarian, you could substitute tofu for the chicken.

COCONUT & TURMERIC CHICKEN CURRY WITH ROASTED PUMPKIN

SERVES **6**
PREPARATION **30 MINUTES**   COOKING **30 MINUTES**

500 g (1 lb 2 oz) jap or kent pumpkin
6 tablespoons vegetable oil
270 ml (9½ fl oz) tin coconut milk
270 ml (9½ fl oz) tin coconut cream
6 kaffir lime leaves
800 g (1 lb 12 oz) skinless free-range chicken breast fillets
1 tablespoon fish sauce
1 tablespoon light brown sugar
½ teaspoon sea salt
juice of 1 lime, plus extra lime wedges, to serve
250 g (9 oz) cherry tomatoes, cut in half
6 kale stalks, leaves roughly chopped
3 tablespoons fried shallots (from Asian stores)
½ bunch (45 g/1½ oz) coriander (cilantro), leaves and stalks roughly chopped

CURRY PASTE

1 little finger–sized piece of fresh turmeric, or 1 teaspoon ground turmeric
1 thumb-sized piece of fresh ginger
1 lemongrass stem, pale part only
2 garlic cloves, peeled
1 large red chilli
2 red Asian shallots, peeled

Preheat the oven to 180°C (350°F). Line a baking tray with baking paper.

Peel the pumpkin, chop into large chunks and place on the baking tray. Drizzle with 2 tablespoons of the vegetable oil and season with sea salt and freshly ground black pepper. Bake for 20 minutes, or until the pumpkin is soft.

To make the curry paste, peel the turmeric and ginger and roughly chop, along with the lemongrass. Place in a food processor, add the remaining ingredients and blend to a paste; alternatively, you could pound to a paste using a mortar and pestle.

In a heavy-based saucepan or flameproof casserole dish, heat the remaining vegetable oil over medium–high heat. Add the curry paste and cook, stirring, for 5 minutes, until the oil has split out of the paste. Turn the heat down to medium, add the coconut milk, coconut cream and lime leaves and cook gently for a further 5 minutes.

Slice the chicken into thin strips. Add to the pan, mixing the sauce through, then cook with the lid on for 8 minutes. It is very important at this point that the sauce is just ticking over very slowly, as you want the chicken to poach gently so it is lovely and tender.

Now stir in the fish sauce, sugar, salt and lime juice, then check the seasoning. Add the pumpkin, cherry tomatoes and kale and cook for a further 5 minutes.

Serve sprinkled with the fried shallots and coriander, with lime wedges and steamed rice on the side.

> *Here we are, at one of my all-time favourite dishes. All the Logue family cook this one. We affectionately call it our 'Friday night' tuna pasta, even though we also eat it on Monday nights, Tuesday nights, Sunday nights and even Saturdays! It gained its 'Friday night' nickname as it's always been our go-to meal when we arrive home late after a huge week at work and play. It's the easiest dish on the planet, and one of the quickest and tastiest too — and all the ingredients can be found in the pantry. It's a real keeper.*

OUR FRIDAY-NIGHT TUNA PASTA

SERVES **4**
PREPARATION **10 MINUTES**   COOKING **15 MINUTES**

3 tablespoons olive oil, plus extra for drizzling (optional)
1 brown onion, finely chopped
1 garlic clove, crushed
2 fresh bay leaves
400 g (14 oz) tin chopped tomatoes
45 g (1½ oz/¼ cup) black or green olives
1 tablespoon baby salted capers, rinsed
1 teaspoon sugar
½ teaspoon sea salt
425 g (15 oz) tin good-quality tuna with chilli
10 basil leaves
2 tablespoons chopped flat-leaf (Italian) parsley
zest of 1 lemon, plus extra to garnish
juice of ½ lemon
500 g (1 lb 2 oz) packet of spaghetti
Labneh (Toolbox, page 28), to serve (optional)

Heat 2 tablespoons of the olive oil in a large heavy-based frying pan or saucepan. Sauté the onion, garlic and bay leaves over medium–high heat for 5 minutes, or until softened and fragrant. Stir in the tomatoes, olives, capers, sugar and salt. Cook over low heat for 10 minutes.

Turn the heat off, then add the tuna, basil and parsley. Gently break up the tuna (I like to leave it quite chunky), mixing it through the sauce when the heat is off so the tuna doesn't dry out; it should just warm through with the residual heat of the sauce. Add the lemon zest, lemon juice and a good grind of black pepper, then check the seasoning.

Meanwhile, cook the spaghetti according to the packet instructions, until al dente. Drain the spaghetti and toss the remaining tablespoon of olive oil through. While the spaghetti is still hot, add it to the sauce and fold through.

Transfer to warm shallow bowls and sprinkle with extra lemon zest. Serve each bowl with a dollop of labneh on top if you have it on hand, and an extra drizzle of olive oil if desired.

Lamb shoulder is a wonderful cut for slow braising as there is enough fat and good muscle in it to keep the meat succulent and moist. The preserved lemon is quite an important flavour ingredient, so please don't leave it out.

MOROCCAN LAMB TAGINE WITH PRESERVED LEMON, FIG & EGGPLANT

SERVES **8**
PREPARATION **45 MINUTES**   COOKING **2½ HOURS**

2 eggplants (aubergines), diced
olive oil, for drizzling and pan-frying
2 red capsicums (peppers), diced
1 kg (2 lb 4 oz) diced lamb shoulder
2 brown onions, diced
2 garlic cloves, crushed
1 celery stalk, roughly chopped
1 carrot, roughly chopped
1 thumb-sized piece of ginger, grated
1 bunch (90 g/3¼ oz) coriander
    (cilantro), roots washed and chopped;
    leaves and stalks chopped separately
4 fresh bay leaves
3 cinnamon sticks
6 cardamom pods, crushed
6 cloves
1 tablespoon ground cumin
1 tablespoon sweet paprika
1 teaspoon ground turmeric
2 tablespoons tomato paste
    (concentrated purée)
400 g (14 oz) tin chopped tomatoes
500 ml (17 fl oz/2 cups) chicken stock
½ Preserved lemon (Toolbox, page 27),
    pulp discarded, skin finely chopped
125 g (4½ oz) dried figs, chopped
2 tablespoons chopped mint
1 teaspoon sea salt

Preheat the oven to 180°C (350°F). Line a baking tray with baking paper.

Spread the eggplant and capsicum on the baking tray and drizzle with 4 tablespoons olive oil. Season with sea salt and freshly ground black pepper and bake for 15 minutes, or until a little caramelised. Remove from the oven and set aside.

Meanwhile, heat 2 tablespoons olive oil in a heavy-based saucepan or flameproof casserole dish over high heat. Brown the lamb in two batches, for about 5 minutes each time, or until browned all over. Remove to a plate and set aside.

In the same pan, heat another 2 tablespoons olive oil over medium–high heat, then stir in the onion, garlic, celery and carrot. Add the ginger, coriander root, bay leaves, cinnamon sticks, cardamom, cloves and ground spices and sauté for 5 minutes, or until the vegetables are soft. Stir in the tomato paste and cook for a further 2 minutes.

Return the lamb to the pan, along with any collected juices. Stir in the tomato, stock and preserved lemon. Cover with a piece of baking paper; this is called a cartouche and helps retain the moisture level in the tagine. Put the lid on, then cook as slowly as your stovetop will allow for 1½ hours. Add the figs and roasted eggplant and capsicum and cook for a further 30 minutes.

Just before serving, stir in the mint, salt and chopped coriander leaves and stalks. Serve with couscous or rice.

CHICKEN PHO NOODLE SOUP

SERVES 8
PREPARATION 1 HOUR + OVERNIGHT CHILLING   COOKING 2½ HOURS

PHO BROTH

2 brown onions, unpeeled

1 thumb-sized piece of fresh ginger, unpeeled

1.6 kg (3 lb 8 oz) whole free-range chicken

1 kg (2 lb 4 oz) chicken bones; necks and wings are good too

1½ tablespoons sea salt

3 tablespoons fish sauce

2.5 cm (1 inch) chunk of yellow rock sugar (from Asian stores)

2 tablespoons coriander seeds, lightly toasted in a dry frying pan for about 1 minute, until fragrant

4 whole cloves

½ bunch (45 g/1½ oz) coriander (cilantro), roots and stalks

FOR THE PHO BROTH

Place the onions and ginger directly on a gas burner or under a hot grill (broiler). Use tongs to rotate the onions and ginger occasionally, to get an even charring. This is a very important step to get the unique flavour of the pho. After 15–20 minutes, the onions and ginger will have softened slightly and become sweetly fragrant. Leave to cool.

Rinse the cooled onions under warm running water, rubbing off the charred skin. Discard the blackened root and stem ends. Now remove the ginger skin using a vegetable peeler, paring knife or the edge of a teaspoon, then rinse the ginger under warm water to wash off any blackened bits. Halve the ginger lengthways and bruise lightly with the broad side of a cleaver or chef's knife. Set the onions and ginger aside.

Rinse the whole chicken under cool water. Cut off the wings and neck, if present, and add to the other chicken bones.

Remove and discard any loose pieces of fat from the chicken bits. With the heel of a large chopping knife, whack the bones to partly cut them through at about 5 cm (2 inch) intervals. This will maximise the flavour you'll get from the bones into your stock. Wash the bones and drain, then place in a large stockpot. Cover with cold water and bring to the boil over high heat. Boil vigorously for 2–3 minutes to release the impurities, then drain the bones and wash.

Clean the saucepan and put the chicken bones back in. Sit the whole chicken on top, breast side up. Pour in 5 litres (175 fl oz/20 cups) water and make sure all the chicken is submerged. Bring to the boil over high heat, then reduce the heat to a gentle simmer. Use a ladle or large, shallow spoon to skim off any scum that rises to the top. Add the onions, ginger, salt, fish sauce, rock sugar, coriander seeds, cloves and coriander roots and stalks. Cook, uncovered, for 25 minutes, keeping the heat at a gentle simmer. At this point, the chicken should be cooked; its flesh should feel firm, yet still yield a little to the touch. Use a pair of tongs to grab the chicken and transfer it to a large bowl. Meanwhile, keep the broth at a steady simmer.

When the chicken is cool enough to handle, use a knife to remove each breast half, and the whole legs (drumsticks and thighs). Leave to cool completely, then cover with plastic wrap and refrigerate; bring to room temperature just before assembling the bowls.

Return the leftover chicken carcass to the stockpot, adjust the heat and simmer the broth gently for another 1½ hours. Avoid cooking the broth at a hard boil, or it will turn cloudy. Set a fine-mesh sieve, or a colander lined with cheesecloth (muslin), over a large pan. Strain the broth through. Discard the solids and refrigerate the stock overnight.

The next day, lift off the solid fat that has set on top, and you'll be left with about 4 litres (140 fl oz/16 cups) of a beautifully clear stock.

TO ASSEMBLE THE PHO BOWLS

Peel the onion, then cut into paper-thin slices. Soak in a small bowl of cold water for 30 minutes. Meanwhile, put the dried noodles in a heatproof bowl, cover with hot tap water and soak for 15–20 minutes, or until pliable and opaque. Drain the onion and noodles and set aside.

Slice the cooked chicken breasts, and cut the leg meat off the bones; set aside. Arrange the garnishes on a plate and place on the table.

To ensure good timing, bring the broth to a simmer over medium heat as you are assembling the bowls. At the same time, fill a large saucepan with water and bring to a rolling boil.

For each bowl, place a good handful of the noodles on a vertical-handle strainer and dunk the noodles in the boiling water. As soon as they have softened, about 20 seconds, pull the strainer from the water. Empty the noodles into serving bowls. Top each bowl with the chicken, soaked onion slices, spring onion and a sprinkling of white pepper.

Increase the heat and bring the broth to a rolling boil. Check your seasoning; you may want to add more salt, fish sauce or sugar. Ladle about 500 ml (17 fl oz/2 cups) broth into each bowl, distributing the hot liquid evenly to warm all the ingredients. Serve immediately, with the plate of garnishes for people to help themselves to.

FOR THE BOWLS
1 brown onion
375 g (13 oz) thin dried flat rice noodles
2 spring onions (scallions), chopped
ground white pepper, for sprinkling

TO GARNISH
8 coriander (cilantro) sprigs
8 Vietnamese mint sprigs
4 spring onions (scallions), thinly sliced
350 g (12 oz/3 cups) bean sprouts
1 lemon, cut into 8 wedges

BRAISED LAMB SHOULDER WITH ARTICHOKE, OLIVES & EGGPLANT

SERVES **8**
PREPARATION **15 MINUTES**   COOKING **2½ HOURS**

olive oil, for pan-frying and drizzling
2 brown onions, roughly chopped
4 garlic cloves, crushed
4 fresh bay leaves
1.4 kg (3 lb 2 oz) boneless lamb shoulder, cut into 4 cm (1½ inch) cubes
2 tablespoons plain (all-purpose) flour
2 tablespoons tomato paste (concentrated purée)
250 ml (9 fl oz/1 cup) white wine
500 ml (17 fl oz/2 cups) chicken stock
400 g (14 oz) tin whole tomatoes
400 g (14 oz) jar artichoke hearts
150 g (5½ oz) black or green olives
2 teaspoons dried oregano
1 eggplant (aubergine), cut into large dice
1 tablespoon sweet paprika
2 tablespoons chopped flat-leaf (Italian) parsley

In a large heavy-based saucepan or flameproof casserole dish, heat 2 tablespoons olive oil over medium–high heat. Add the onion, garlic and bay leaves and sauté for 5 minutes, or until the onion is softened and fragrant. Remove from the pan and set aside.

Toss the lamb in the flour and season with sea salt and freshly ground black pepper. Heat another 2 tablespoons olive oil in the pan over high heat, then brown the lamb in two batches, turning until the meat has browned all over. Add the tomato paste and allow to cook out for 2 minutes.

Add the wine and stir well to deglaze the pan. Stir in the stock, tomatoes, artichoke hearts, olives, oregano and the sautéed onion. Place the lid on, then cook as slowly as your stovetop will allow for 1½ hours.

Meanwhile, preheat the oven to 180°C (350°F). Line a baking tray with baking paper, spread the eggplant on the tray and drizzle with 2 tablespoons olive oil. Sprinkle with the paprika and season with salt and pepper, then bake for 15–20 minutes, or until the eggplant has caramelised slightly. Remove from the oven and set aside until needed.

After the lamb has been braising for 1½ hours, stir in the baked eggplant and the parsley. Pop the lid back on and cook for a further 30 minutes.

Check the seasoning and serve with rice or mashed potato.

CHICKEN, TOMATO & OLIVE DUMPLINGS WITH FETA & KALE

SERVES **6–8**
PREPARATION **30 MINUTES**   COOKING **1½ HOURS**

TOMATO SAUCE

2 tablespoons olive oil
1 onion, chopped
1 garlic clove, chopped
2 tablespoons tomato paste
   (concentrated purée)
2 x 400 g (14 oz) tins chopped tomato
500 ml (17 fl oz/2 cups) chicken stock
1 tablespoon sugar
1 teaspoon sea salt
3 fresh bay leaves

DUMPLINGS

1 kg (2 lb 4 oz) minced (ground) chicken
60 g (2¼ oz/1 cup) fresh sourdough
   breadcrumbs (see Tip)
1 free-range egg, lightly beaten
1 onion, finely chopped
2 garlic cloves, crushed
75 g (2½ oz/½ cup) sun-dried tomatoes,
   chopped
95 g (3¼ oz/½ cup) kalamata olives,
   pitted and chopped
45 g (1½ oz/½ cup) grated parmesan
2 tablespoons chopped basil
2 tablespoons chopped parsley
2 teaspoons sea salt
1 teaspoon freshly ground black pepper
1 tablespoon sweet paprika

FOR THE KALE

6–8 leafy kale stalks
2 tablespoons olive oil
1 garlic clove, chopped
juice of 1 lemon
150 g (5½ oz) feta cheese, crumbled

Start by making the tomato sauce. In a heavy-based saucepan large enough to hold the sauce and all the dumplings, heat the olive oil. Add the onion and sauté over medium heat for 5 minutes, or until fragrant. Add the garlic and cook for a further 1 minute, then stir in the tomato paste, tomatoes, stock, sugar, salt and bay leaves. Cook nice and slowly for 1 hour, until the sauce becomes lovely and rich.

Meanwhile, preheat the oven to 180°C (350°F) and line a large baking tray with baking paper. Place all the dumpling ingredients, except the paprika, in a large bowl and mix with your hands to combine. Using wet hands to stop the mixture sticking, roll it into walnut-sized balls, placing them on the baking tray. Sprinkle the dumplings with the paprika, then bake for 15 minutes, or until cooked through. Do not overcook; the dumplings should be lovely and moist. Remove from the oven and set aside, leaving them on the tray.

When the tomato sauce is ready, add the dumplings and any juices that have collected on the tray. Cook slowly, leaving the lid off, for a further 15 minutes, stirring occasionally.

Just before serving, prepare the kale. Strip the leaves off the stalks, discarding the stalks. Give the leaves a good wash, then roughly chop. Warm the olive oil in a large frying pan over medium heat and sauté the garlic for 1 minute, or until fragrant. Carefully add the chopped kale, standing back a little as the oil will spit. Turn the kale with a pair of tongs and drizzle with the lemon juice, then cook for 5 minutes, or until the kale has wilted down and is a super-vibrant green.

Serve the dumplings and tomato sauce topped with the kale and feta.

TIP: Whenever I have left-over bits of sourdough bread, I turn them into breadcrumbs and bag them up in the freezer for dishes like this. It's also great to make a double batch of these dumplings and get the ones you love to help you roll them. The extra dumplings will freeze brilliantly for an emergency dinner later on.

With sweet bursts of caramelised garlic and a nice mellow warmth from the green peppercorns, this is a great braise in winter. You can cook it slowly in the oven, or keep it ticking along on the stove. Serve with buttery noodles or creamy mash.

BRAISED BEEF WITH GREEN PEPPERCORNS & ROASTED GARLIC

SERVES **6**
PREPARATION **30 MINUTES**   COOKING **2 HOURS**

---

1 garlic bulb, cloves separated and peeled
4 tablespoons olive oil
1 kg (2 lb 4 oz) chuck steak; ask your butcher to cut it into 4 cm (1½ inch) cubes, and leave about 10% of fat on the cut, to keep the beef moist during the slow braising
60 ml (2 fl oz/¼ cup) brandy
2 brown onions, diced
2 carrots, diced
2 celery stalks, diced
4 fresh bay leaves
2 tablespoons tomato paste (concentrated purée)
1 litre (35 fl oz/4 cups) beef stock
4 large field mushrooms, sliced
1 tablespoon green peppercorns
50 g (1¾ oz) salted butter
50 g (1¾ oz/⅓ cup) plain (all-purpose) flour
150 g (5½ oz) baby English spinach leaves

Preheat the oven to 160°C (315°F). Place the garlic cloves in a piece of foil, with 1 tablespoon of the olive oil and a sprinkling of sea salt and freshly ground black pepper. Fold up into a well-sealed parcel and bake for 20 minutes, or until the garlic is soft, nutty and caramelised. Set aside, leaving the oven on if braising the beef in the oven.

Meanwhile, warm a large heavy-based saucepan or flameproof casserole dish on the stove over medium–high heat. Add 1½ tablespoons of the remaining olive oil. Season the beef with salt and pepper and cook in batches for about 5 minutes each time, until caramelised all over, removing each batch to a large dish. When all the beef is done, splash the brandy into the pan and give it a good stir to deglaze all the stuck-on bits. Pour the brandied pan juices over the beef.

Clean out the saucepan or casserole dish and place back over medium–high heat. Add the remaining olive oil. Sauté the onion, carrot, celery and bay leaves for 5 minutes, or until the vegetables are softened and caramelised. Stir in the tomato paste and cook for another 2 minutes. Return the beef to the pan, along with all the juices that have collected in the dish, and cook for 5 minutes. Stir in the stock, mushrooms and peppercorns, then cover with a lid. Turn the heat right down to low, or transfer to the oven, if using. Leave to simmer gently for 1½ hours, or until the meat has softened.

In a small saucepan, melt the butter over low heat, then stir in the flour until smooth. Stir with a wooden spoon for 5 minutes to cook out the flour taste, then stir the roux into the stew, along with the caramelised garlic and the spinach leaves. Leave to thicken for about 10 minutes, then check the seasoning and serve.

This recipe, along with many others, was a gift from my brother Andy. For easy entertaining, the ragout can be cooked a day or two ahead — refrigerate until needed, then scrape the congealed fat from the top of the stew before gently reheating it. The gnocchi can also be shaped a few hours ahead and cooked just before serving.

GNOCCHI WITH OXTAIL RAGOUT

SERVES **8**
PREPARATION **40 MINUTES**   COOKING **2½ HOURS**

1 tomato, diced
1 bunch (150 g/5½ oz) flat-leaf (Italian)
    parsley, leaves chopped
juice of 1 lemon
grated or shaved parmesan cheese,
    to serve

OXTAIL RAGOUT

2 kg (4 lb 8 oz) oxtail pieces
100 ml (3½ fl oz) brandy
2 tablespoons olive oil
1 onion, chopped
4 garlic cloves, chopped
2 carrots, diced
2 celery stalks, diced
100 g (3½ oz) speck or smoked bacon,
    chopped
2 fresh bay leaves
4 thyme sprigs
½ teaspoon freshly grated nutmeg
3 tablespoons tomato paste
    (concentrated purée)
250 ml (9 fl oz/1 cup) good red wine
500 ml (17 fl oz/2 cups) beef stock

POTATO GNOCCHI

1 kg (2 lb 4 oz) floury (roasting) potatoes
1 free-range egg yolk, lightly beaten
150 g (5½ oz/1 cup) plain (all-purpose)
    flour
1 teaspoon sea salt

FOR THE OXTAIL RAGOUT

Preheat the oven to 200°C (400°F). Heat a heavy-based saucepan or flameproof casserole dish over medium–high heat. Working in batches, brown the oxtail on all sides; you won't need any oil as the oxtail is quite fatty. Transfer each batch to a dish. Deglaze the pan with the brandy, then pour the brandied pan juices over the oxtail.

Place the pan back over medium heat. Add the olive oil, then sauté the onion and garlic for 5 minutes, until golden. Add the carrot, celery, speck, herbs and nutmeg. Season with sea salt and freshly ground black pepper and sauté for a further 5 minutes. Stir in the tomato paste.

Place the oxtail back in the pan; pour in the wine and stock. Put the lid on, then braise in the oven for 2 hours, or until the meat is tender. Remove the oxtail from the pan, then strain the sauce into a clean saucepan. Take the meat off the bone and add it to the sauce. Keep warm, or refrigerate until needed and reheat for serving.

FOR THE POTATO GNOCCHI

Wash the potatoes well, leaving the skins on. Steam for 30 minutes, or until tender. Cool slightly, then peel. While they are still warm, pass the potatoes through a potato ricer, onto a floured workbench. Make a well in the centre, add the egg yolk and flour and knead until well combined. Using your hands, roll the gnocchi mixture into a thin sausage about 2 cm (¾ inch) thick. Cut into small pieces about 1 cm (½ inch) thick.

TO SERVE

In small batches, drop the gnocchi into a large pot of lightly salted boiling water. As they rise to the surface, scoop them out with a slotted spoon. Fold them through the oxtail sauce, along with the diced tomato, parsley and lemon juice. Serve garnished with parmesan.

*My friend Dominique introduced me to hedgehog potatoes. What a discovery!
It seemed only natural to team them with a delicious chicken schnitzel and
a perky rocket salad. This combo is absolutely delicious.*

HERBIE CHICKEN SCHNITZELS WITH HEDGEHOG POTATOES

SERVES **4**
PREPARATION **40 MINUTES** COOKING **1 HOUR**

SCHNITZELS

4 x 160 g (5½ oz) skinless free-range
  chicken breast fillets
250 g (9 oz/4 cups) fresh sourdough
  breadcrumbs
3 thyme sprigs
2 tablespoons chopped flat-leaf (Italian)
  parsley
45 g (1½ oz/½ cup) grated parmesan
  cheese
zest of 1 lemon
2 garlic cloves, finely chopped
2 tablespoons sesame seeds
2 teaspoons sea salt
2 free-range eggs
125 ml (4 fl oz/½ cup) milk
225 g (8 oz/1½ cups) plain (all-purpose)
  flour
100 ml (3½ fl oz) olive oil
50 g (1¾ oz) butter

FOR THE SCHNITZELS

Preheat the oven to 180°C (350°F). Line a baking tray with
baking paper.

Using a sharp knife, cut through each chicken breast horizontally,
but not all the way through; we call this 'butterflying'. Open the
breasts out and lay them on a tray.

In a large bowl, combine the breadcrumbs, thyme, parsley, parmesan,
lemon zest, garlic, sesame seeds, salt and a sprinkling of freshly ground
black pepper. In another bowl, whisk together the eggs and milk. Put
the flour in a third bowl and season with a little salt and pepper.

You are now ready to crumb the chicken. To avoid really messy fingers,
the trick to remember is to use one hand for the dry ingredients, and
the other hand for the wet ingredients. Dust one chicken breast all
over with the flour, then dip it in the egg, allowing the excess to drip
off. Finally, press it into the breadcrumbs, making sure it is evenly
coated. Lay the chicken breast on a plate, repeat with the remaining
ingredients and set aside.

Heat the olive oil and butter in a large heavy-based frying pan over
medium–high heat. When the butter starts to foam, add two chicken
schnitzels and cook for 3 minutes on each side, or until they are nice
and golden and crispy. Drain on paper towel, then place on the
prepared baking tray. Repeat with the remaining two schnitzels.

Place in the oven for 10 minutes to fully cook through.

FOR THE HEDGEHOGS

Preheat the oven to 180°C (350°F). Line a flat baking tray with baking paper. Spray the lined tray quite liberally with olive oil spray.

Meanwhile, put the potatoes in a saucepan, cover with cold water and add a pinch of salt. Bring to the boil, then cook for 20 minutes, or until just tender. Drain and leave to dry.

When the potatoes are cool enough to handle, carefully peel them and cut each one in half. Lay the potatoes on the baking tray, cut side down. Using a fork, carefully scratch the upper side so they look like little baby spiky hedgehogs. Spray with olive oil spray and season liberally with sea salt. Bake for 40 minutes, or until the hedgehogs are all golden and crunchy and fluffy on the inside.

TO SERVE

Toss the rocket salad ingredients together. In a separate small serving bowl, combine the lemon mayonnaise ingredients.

Serve the schnitzels and hedgehog potatoes hot from the oven, with the rocket salad and lemon mayo on the side.

TIP: You can crumb the schnitzels a few hours ahead. Store them in the fridge, with baking paper between each one, covered with plastic wrap. Near serving time, leave them at room temperature for 5 minutes to take the chill off before you pan-fry them; then, when the hedgehogs are nearly done, pop the schnitzels in the oven for the final 10 minutes to cook through.

HEDGEHOGS

8 medium-sized, oval-shaped roasting
   potatoes, such as King Edward, skin on
olive oil spray

ROCKET SALAD

2 bunches (300 g/10½ oz) rocket
   (arugula)
1 quantity Lemon, garlic & dijon dressing
   (Toolbox, page 17)

LEMON MAYONNAISE

120 g (4¼ oz/½ cup) Mayonnaise
   (Toolbox, page 13)
zest and juice of ½ lemon

Chapter Seven

PIES & PASTRIES

AS MY CAKE-BAKING BUSINESS GREW,
IT SEEMED NATURAL TO BRANCH OUT
INTO 'HOME MEAL THERAPY' AS WELL.

But this left, for a while, a missing link. I used to buy other people's pies into my stores to on-sell to customers — until one day I had an epiphany: why shouldn't I make my own?

So I bought a 'dough break' machine, which is like a huge pasta-making machine, and asked the man who sold me my flour and sugar to show me how to use it. On that day our iconic pies were born.

Nowadays I sell hundreds of thousands of pies each year to the airline and grocery sectors. Sometimes I'll bring one home for dinner, and when I sit down to eat it and remember the early days, I think to myself, 'Damn this is a good pie!'

> *When it comes to pizza, I'm a real 'thin crust' kind of girl, and with the toppings, I always feel that less is more. This is one of my favourites — the sweetness of the pumpkin, sharpness of feta and the delicate crunch of aromatic fresh sage as it crisps up in a hot oven is a wonderful combination. If you can get hold of a terracotta tile, it's really great to heat it up in the oven, then cook your pizza on top of it for a crisper crust.*

PIZZA WITH ROASTED PUMPKIN, FETA & SAGE

MAKES **3 PIZZAS**; SERVES **6**
PREPARATION **1 HOUR**   COOKING **50 MINUTES**

600 g (1 lb 5 oz) pumpkin (winter squash), peeled and sliced into 1 cm (½ inch) wedges
4 tablespoons olive oil
½ quantity Pizza dough (Toolbox, page 33)
300 g (10½ oz) mozzarella cheese, shredded
150 g (5½ oz) feta cheese, crumbled
20 fresh sage leaves, approximately

TOMATO SAUCE
2 tablespoons olive oil
1 onion, finely diced
2 garlic cloves, crushed
2 fresh bay leaves
1 tablespoon tomato paste (concentrated purée)
500 g (1 lb 2 oz) tomato sugo, passata, or chopped tinned tomatoes
1 teaspoon sea salt
1 teaspoon sugar
4 tablespoons chopped basil

Preheat the oven to 180°C (350°F). Line two baking trays with baking paper. Place the pumpkin wedges on the trays and season with sea salt and freshly ground black pepper. Drizzle with the olive oil and bake for 20–30 minutes, or until just tender.

To make the tomato sauce, heat the olive oil in a heavy-based saucepan over medium heat. Sauté the onion, garlic and bay leaves for 5 minutes, or until the onion is fragrant and soft. Stir in the tomato paste and cook for 2 minutes. Add the tomato sugo and cook slowly, stirring now and then, for 30 minutes. Stir in the salt, sugar and basil and set aside. (You won't need all the sauce, but the leftover sauce can be used in pasta dishes and stews; it will keep in the fridge for up to 1 week, or can be frozen for up to 3 months.)

When you're ready to eat, preheat the oven to 200°C (400°F). Grease three large pizza trays.

Divide the pizza dough into three balls. Roll them out a little, then stretch them out onto the trays. Spoon 3 tablespoons of the tomato sauce onto each pizza and spread to the outside edges. Evenly scatter half the mozzarella over each pizza. Top with the roasted pumpkin wedges, feta and sage, and a sprinkling of salt and pepper.

Bake for 15–20 minutes, or until the dough is cooked and the cheesy top is all gooey and golden. Serve hot.

On a chilly night, there's nothing more nurturing than this creamy pie. At the shop, we bake little individual pies, and they just walk out the door. At home, I like to bake a big one in a shallow casserole dish, so the béchamel bubbles up into the cheesy topping, creating golden crunchy bits.

SALMON PIE WITH CHEESY POTATO TOP

SERVES **4–6**
PREPARATION **45 MINUTES**   COOKING **50 MINUTES**

2 tablespoons olive oil
50 g (1¾ oz) salted butter
2 leeks, pale part only, chopped
1 large carrot, chopped
1 celery stalk, chopped
4 fresh bay leaves
50 g (1¾ oz/⅓ cup) plain (all-purpose) flour
1 tablespoon dijon mustard
1 litre (35 fl oz/4 cups) milk
1 kg (2 lb 4 oz) salmon, pin boned, skin removed and cut into chunks
zest and juice of 1 lemon
2 tablespoons chopped dill
140 g (5 oz/1 cup) frozen green peas
1 teaspoon sea salt
¼ teaspoon ground white pepper
lemon wedges, to serve

CHEESY POTATO TOPPING
1 kg (2 lb 4 oz) floury (roasting) potatoes
50 g (1¾ oz) salted butter, at room temperature
50 ml (1¾ fl oz) thin (pouring/whipping) cream
100 g (3½ oz/1 cup) grated gruyère cheese

Preheat the oven to 180°C (350°F). Grease a large shallow baking dish.

Start by preparing the topping. Peel the potatoes and cut into chunks. Place in a saucepan, cover with warm water and bring to the boil. Reduce the heat and simmer for 20 minutes, or until the potato is tender. Drain the potato, then add the butter and cream and mash until light and fluffy. Place in a glass bowl and set aside.

Meanwhile, heat the olive oil and butter in a large heavy-based saucepan or flameproof casserole dish over medium heat. Add the leek, carrot, celery and bay leaves and cook for 10 minutes, or until the vegetables have softened. Stir in the flour and mustard until smooth, then cook for 3 minutes. Add the milk and stir with a wooden spoon for 5 minutes, or until the mixture has thickened. Turn the heat down low, then fold in the salmon, lemon zest, lemon juice, dill and peas. Season with sea salt and freshly ground black pepper, place the lid on and cook gently for 5 minutes.

Add the fish mixture to the greased baking dish, then top with the mashed potato and scatter with the gruyère cheese.

Bake for 30 minutes, or until the topping is golden. Serve hot, with lemon wedges and a crisp green salad.

TIP: It's easier to spread the mashed potato if it's hot, so if preparing it in advance, give it a zap in the microwave to soften it before topping the pie.

I love cooking this rich and hearty pie in the depths of winter, with a fire flickering away in the hearth and a nice bottle of Shiraz at hand. Serve the pie with a potato mash — it doesn't get much better than that.

BEEF & GUINNESS PIE WITH SOUR CREAM PASTRY

SERVES **6**
PREPARATION **30 MINUTES**   COOKING **2 HOURS + 40 MINUTES BAKING**

1 quantity Sour cream pastry (Toolbox, page 34), rested and chilled
1 free-range egg, whisked with
    2 tablespoons milk

FOR THE FILLING
800 g (1 lb 12 oz) chuck steak, cut into
    4 cm (1½ inch) cubes
4 tablespoons plain (all-purpose) flour
4 tablespoons olive oil
300 ml (10½ fl oz) Guinness
2 brown onions, sliced
1 garlic clove, crushed
1 celery stalk, diced
1 large carrot, diced
2 fresh bay leaves
2 tablespoons tomato paste
    (concentrated purée)
250 ml (9 fl oz/1 cup) beef stock

Start by making the filling. Toss the beef in the flour and season with sea salt and freshly ground black pepper. Heat half the olive oil in a large heavy-based saucepan or flameproof casserole dish, then cook the beef in batches over medium–high heat for 5 minutes, or until browned all over. Remove to a bowl.

Pour the beer into the pan and give it a good stir to deglaze the pan. Let the beer bubble away for 2 minutes to bring up all the goodness from the bottom of the pan. Pour the beery pan juices over the beef.

Heat the remaining olive oil in the pan, then sauté the onion, garlic, celery, carrot and bay leaves for 10 minutes, or until soft and fragrant. Stir in the tomato paste and cook for a further 2 minutes. Return the beef to the pan, along with all the beery juices. Pour in the stock and pop on the lid. Cook over low heat for 2 hours, or until the meat is very tender and the sauce is lovely and thick. Place the mixture in a bowl, cover and refrigerate until cool; overnight would even be better, to allow the flavours to develop.

When you're ready to bake the pie, preheat the oven to 200°C (400°F) and grease a 23 cm (9 inch) pie dish. On a lightly floured workbench, roll out half the pastry to about 5 mm (¼ inch) thick, then ease the pastry into the pie dish. Fill the pie with the chilled beef mixture. Roll out the remaining pastry to about 5 mm (¼ inch) thick, then carefully place it on top of the pie. Using your fingers or a fork, press the top and bottom pastry edges together to seal them. Trim the pastry edges, then prick the centre with a fork to let the steam escape.

Brush the top of the pie with the beaten egg mixture and bake for 35–40 minutes, or until the pastry is golden.

CHICKEN & LEEK PIES WITH SCRUNCHED & BUTTERY FILO TOPS

MAKES **12 SMALL PIES**; SERVES **6 FOR DINNER**, OR **12 FOR BRUNCH**
PREPARATION **30 MINUTES**   COOKING **25 MINUTES + 30 MINUTES BAKING**

1 quantity Sour cream pastry (Toolbox, page 34)

375 g (13 oz) packet filo pastry; you'll need 18 sheets, measuring about 45 cm x 26 cm (17½ inches x 10½ inches)

200 g (7 oz) salted butter, melted

FOR THE FILLING

1 tablespoon olive oil

500 g (1 lb 2 oz) skinless free-range chicken thigh fillets, cut into 5 cm (2 inch) chunks

2 tablespoons salted butter

2 leeks, pale part only, thinly sliced

1 garlic clove, crushed

2 fresh bay leaves

3 tablespoons plain (all-purpose) flour

125 ml (4 fl oz/½ cup) full-cream milk

250 ml (9 fl oz/1 cup) thin (pouring/whipping) cream

1½ teaspoons sea salt

¼ teaspoon ground white pepper

2 tablespoons chopped flat-leaf (Italian) parsley

To make the filling, heat the olive oil in a heavy-based saucepan over medium heat. Sauté the chicken in two batches for 5 minutes each time, or until cooked through, then remove to a plate. Melt the butter in the pan over medium heat. Sauté the leek, garlic and bay leaves for 5–10 minutes, or until soft and fragrant. Stir in the flour and cook for 3 minutes, then stir in the milk and cream and cook for 2 minutes. Return the chicken to the pan, along with any juices. Stir in the salt, white pepper and parsley. Transfer to a bowl, cover and refrigerate until cool; the filling can be made a day ahead, if needed.

Preheat the oven to 180°C (350°F). Grease 12 pie dishes, each 10 cm (4 inches) wide and 2 cm (¾ inch) deep. (Alternatively, you can make one big pie in a 23 cm/9 inch shallow pie dish.)

On a lightly floured workbench, roll out the sour cream pastry to about 8 mm (⅜ inch) thick. Use an 11 cm (4¼ inch) pastry cutter to cut out 12 rounds. Ease the pastry into the pie dishes and trim the edges. Fill with the chilled chicken mixture.

Lay the filo pastry on your workbench. Using scissors, cut the pastry in half from top to bottom, so you now have 36 pieces. Cover with a damp tea towel to stop the pastry drying out. Take one piece of filo pastry and brush with the melted butter. Top with another piece, brush with more butter, then top with a third piece of filo and brush with more butter. Scrunch the three pastry layers up and place on top of one of the pies. Repeat with the remaining filo pastry and butter, until you have topped all of the pies.

Brush with the remaining butter and sprinkle with sea salt. Bake for 30 minutes, or until the pies are golden, and the pastry tops crunchy.

The classic topping for pissaladière is anchovy and olive, but I really love our combo of sweet red onion, tangy goat's cheese and fragrant thyme. Serve this tasty tart for lunch with a salad, or cut into smaller pieces to pass around at a cocktail party.

PISSALADIÈRE WITH CARAMELISED ONION, GOAT'S CHEESE & THYME

MAKES 1 LARGE TART: SERVES 6 FOR LUNCH, OR 12 TO PASS AROUND
PREPARATION 40 MINUTES   COOKING 20 MINUTES + 30 MINUTES BAKING

2 tablespoons olive oil

6 red onions, sliced

2 garlic cloves, crushed

2 fresh bay leaves

2 tablespoons balsamic vinegar

1 tablespoon light brown sugar

1 teaspoon sea salt

¼ teaspoon freshly ground black pepper

½ quantity Easy rough puff pastry
   (Toolbox, page 35)

2 tablespoons tomato paste
   (concentrated purée)

300 g (10½ oz/3 cups, loosely packed)
   grated cheddar cheese

150 g (5½ oz/1¼ cups) crumbled goat's
   cheese

12 thyme sprigs, leaves picked

Preheat the oven to 200°C (400°F). Grease a 30 cm x 20 cm (12 inch x 8 inch) baking tray with small raised sides.

In a large non-stick frying pan, heat the olive oil over medium–high heat. Add the onion, garlic and bay leaves and allow to cook down for 10 minutes, or until the onion is soft and fragrant. Add the vinegar, sugar, salt and pepper, then cook for a further 5 minutes, or until the onion has caramelised. Set aside to cool completely.

On a lightly floured workbench, roll out the pastry into a rectangle about 6 mm (¼ inch) thick, and large enough to fit the baking tray. Roll the pastry onto the rolling pin and gently place it over the baking tray. Trim the overhanging pastry and crimp the edges around the outside of the tray. Prick the pastry all over with a fork; this is called 'docking', and helps the pastry bake without puffing up too much.

Bake for 15 minutes, or until the pastry is golden. Remove from the oven and leave until cool enough to handle safely.

Smear the pastry with the tomato paste, then top with the caramelised onion, spreading it evenly over the pastry. Scatter the cheddar over, then dot with the goat's cheese and sprinkle with the thyme leaves.

Bake for a further 10–15 minutes, or until the cheese has melted. Remove from the oven and leave to rest for 10 minutes before cutting.

We bake a lot of spanakopita and our customers love it. My friend and former colleague Joey Kitas taught me about the importance of using fresh dill and a touch of nutmeg. As for the soda water, I know it seems crazy, but it really works. You'll see.

SPANAKOPITA

SERVES **8**
PREPARATION **30 MINUTES**   COOKING **1 HOUR**

2 bunches silverbeet (Swiss chard), about 600 g (1 lb 5 oz) each
6 free-range eggs, lightly beaten
440 g (15½ oz/3⅓ cups) crumbled creamy feta cheese
250 g (9 oz) ricotta cheese
60 g (2¼ oz/1 cup) chopped dill
6 spring onions (scallions), white and light green bits only, chopped
1 teaspoon ground nutmeg
150 g (5½ oz) salted butter
150 ml (5 fl oz) olive oil
375 g (13 oz) packet filo pastry
150 ml (5 fl oz) soda water

Preheat the oven to 180°C (350°F).

Bring a large saucepan of salted water to the boil. Cut out and discard the central white ribs and stalks from the silverbeet. Blanch the leaves, in batches if needed, in the boiling water for 3 minutes. Drain and cool slightly, then squeeze the excess water out and roughly chop.

Place the silverbeet in a large bowl. Add the eggs, feta, ricotta, dill, spring onion and nutmeg and gently mix to combine. Set aside.

In a saucepan, gently melt the butter. Stir in the olive oil and set aside.

Brush a 28 cm x 18 cm (11 inch x 7 inch) baking dish with some of the melted butter mixture. Use half the filo pastry sheets to line the bottom of the baking dish, brushing some of the melted butter mixture between each layer of pastry. Evenly spread the spinach mixture over the filo pastry base. Now layer the remaining filo sheets over the spinach layer, brushing some of the melted butter mixture between each layer of pastry, and over the final layer.

Before baking the pie, use a sharp knife to cut the pie into squares, all the way through; this makes cutting the pie a lot easier once you have cooked it. Transfer to the oven and bake for 15 minutes.

Now for the interesting bit! Remove the pie from the oven and pour the soda water over the top. Reduce the oven temperature to 150°C (300°F) and bake for a further 20–30 minutes, or until the pie has puffed up and the pastry is a lovely golden colour.

Remove the pie from the oven and rest for 10–15 minutes. Serve hot or cold, with a yummy salad.

A lovely pretty green, this tart sings out springtime. Tiny chia seeds are such a great super food, so one day I thought I'd experiment by working some into the shortcrust pastry for this tart, and we all loved it.

ZUCCHINI, FETA & ASPARAGUS TART WITH CHIA PASTRY

SERVES **6–8**
PREPARATION **40 MINUTES**   COOKING **50 MINUTES**

1 quantity Sour cream pastry (Toolbox, page 34), with 3 tablespoons chia seeds added to the flour

2 tablespoons olive oil

2 leeks, pale part only, chopped

1 zucchini, about 150 g (5½ oz), grated

2 tablespoons chopped mint

2 tablespoons chopped chives

6 free-range eggs

200 ml (7 fl oz) thin (pouring/whipping) cream

1 teaspoon sea salt

¼ teaspoon freshly ground black pepper

12 asparagus spears, woody ends trimmed

100 g (3½ oz/1 cup) grated gruyère cheese

100 g (3½ oz/⅔ cup) crumbled feta cheese

Preheat the oven to 180°C (350°F).

On a lightly floured workbench, roll out the pastry to about 8 mm (⅜ inch) thick. Press into a 23 cm (9 inch) loose-based fluted flan (tart) tin and trim the edges. Rest for 20 minutes in the refrigerator.

Line the tart shell with a sheet of baking paper, then fill with baking beads or uncooked rice or dried beans. Bake for 15 minutes. Remove the baking paper and beads, then bake for a further 10 minutes, or until the pastry is golden. Remove the tart shell from the oven; reduce the oven temperature to 150°C (300°F).

While the pastry is blind baking, heat the olive oil in a large non-stick frying pan. Sauté the leek over medium heat for 5–10 minutes, or until soft and fragrant. Remove from the heat and leave to cool.

Spread the cooled leek over the blind-baked tart shell. Squeeze as much water out of the grated zucchini as possible, then arrange on top of the leek. Sprinkle with the mint and chives.

In a bowl, whisk together the eggs, cream, salt and pepper. Pour the mixture over the tart. Lay the asparagus spears on top, then sprinkle with the gruyère and feta.

Bake for 25 minutes, or until the filling is cooked in the centre and the pastry is golden. This tart is lovely served warm, but is wonderful cold as well — great to take to a picnic.

The house never smells better than when you are pulling these beauties, all puffed up and golden, from the oven. Pork and fennel truly are meant to be together forever; the grated apple adds extra moisture and a little perky brightness.

PORK & FENNEL SAUSAGE ROLLS

MAKES 16 LUNCH ROLLS, OR 48 COCKTAIL ROLLS
PREPARATION 30 MINUTES + 1 HOUR RESTING   COOKING 40 MINUTES

2 tablespoons olive oil

2 brown onions, finely chopped

2 garlic cloves, crushed

2 celery stalks, about 150 g (5½ oz), finely chopped

1 large carrot, about 150 g (5½ oz), grated

2 fresh bay leaves

1 kg (2 lb 4 oz) coarsely minced (ground) pork

1 granny smith apple, peeled and grated

125 g (4½ oz/2 cups) fresh sourdough breadcrumbs

3 teaspoons sea salt

½ teaspoon ground white pepper

2 tablespoons fennel seeds, lightly toasted, plus extra for sprinkling

2 free-range eggs

1 quantity Easy rough puff pastry (Toolbox, page 35)

60 ml (2 fl oz/¼ cup) milk

In a large non-stick frying pan, heat the olive oil and sauté the onion, garlic, celery, carrot and bay leaves over medium heat for 5–10 minutes, or until the vegetables have softened and the mixture is fragrant.

Remove the bay leaves, then tip the mixture into a bowl. Add the pork, apple, breadcrumbs, salt, pepper, fennel seeds and one of the eggs. Mix together using your hands for about 5 minutes, really working the protein of the meat. Cover and rest in the refrigerator for 1 hour to let the flavours mingle, or overnight if you have the time.

Preheat the oven to 180°C (350°F). On a lightly floured workbench, roll out half the pastry into a 85 cm x 20 cm (33½ inch x 8 inch) rectangle, about 5 mm (¼ inch) thick. Repeat with the remaining pastry. Divide the pork mixture into two even portions. Place one portion along the middle of one of the pastry rectangles, shaping it into a log.

In a small bowl, whisk the milk with the remaining egg to make an egg wash. Use a pastry brush to brush the egg wash down the long side of the pastry, close to the pork mixture. Fold the pastry over the the filling, then roll it over so the pastry is overlapping; press together. You should only need two-thirds of the pastry in the roll, so trim off the last third. Repeat with the remaining pastry and pork mixture.

Brush the rolls with the remaining egg wash, then sprinkle with extra fennel seeds. You should have about 500 g (1 lb 2 oz) puff pastry left; freeze it for another time to top a pie. (These rolls also freeze really well, if you want to freeze some for later enjoyment.)

Cut your rolls to your desired length — eight 10 cm (4 inch) portions per roll for lunch-size sausage rolls, or 24 portions per roll for cocktail rolls. Place on a greased baking tray and bake for 30 minutes, or until the pastry is golden brown and the filling is cooked.

Chapter Eight

COCKTAIL & PARTY FOOD

CATERING FOR COCKTAIL PARTIES PLAYS A BIG PART IN MY BUSINESS THESE DAYS.

Most Friday and Saturday nights I am privileged to be in someone's home, somewhere in Sydney, preparing cocktails and beautiful little morsels to pass around. Cocktail parties are such a great way to entertain, as everyone can mingle and catch up with each other — so easy, informal and relaxed.

These are my favourite nibbles, as you can do a lot of the preparation in the days leading up to the party, leaving you free on the night to have as much fun as your guests.

Serve these scallops when you want to impress, using the freshest and largest you can find. It is very important not to overcook the scallops or they'll be rubbery, so follow the instructions precisely, and don't be tempted to extend the cooking time. You're after a lovely caramelisation, which comes naturally to the scallop. Also, just cook a few at a time, so they have lots of room in the pan; one turn is all they need.

Presenting each scallop in a spoon works well... but if you come across some fresh betel leaves, they'll take this classy little cocktail item to a whole new level.

SEARED SCALLOPS WITH GREEN MANGO SALAD & NAM JIM

MAKES **20**
PREPARATION **20 MINUTES**   COOKING **5 MINUTES**

---

20 large fresh scallops; if the roe is still
   attached, leave it on
olive oil spray
1 quantity Nam jim (Toolbox, page 19)
35 g (1¼ oz/¼ cup) peanuts, toasted
   and crushed

FOR THE SALAD
2 green mangoes, flesh peeled and finely
   shredded
4 tablespoons finely chopped coriander
   (cilantro)
4 tablespoons finely chopped mint
1 red Asian shallot, peeled and thinly
   sliced
½ red chilli, seeded and finely chopped

In a bowl, toss together all the salad ingredients. Set aside.

Using paper towel, dry the scallops on both sides, then season with sea salt and freshly ground black pepper. Have some more paper towel at the ready.

Place a large non-stick frying pan over medium–high heat and spray with olive oil spray. When the pan is quite hot, add 10 scallops and cook on one side for 1 minute. It is very important that the pan is not overcrowded, or the scallops will not caramelise properly. When the scallops are nicely browned underneath, turn them over and cook for 1 minute on the other side. Remove the scallops from the pan and place on paper towel to rest and release their milky juices.

Cook and rest the remaining scallops in the same way.

Place the warm scallops on little serving spoons and top with the salad. Dress each one with a drizzle of nam jim and a sprinkling of toasted peanuts.

These spidery-looking taste sensations are so popular that when I tried to take them off our catering menu, to mix things up a little, there was an outcry! I just love the look of them piled up on a platter, alongside lots of fresh lime or lemon wedges.

COCONUT PRAWNS WITH SWEET CHILLI & GINGER DIPPING SAUCE

MAKES **20**
PREPARATION **30 MINUTES**   COOKING **35 MINUTES**

150 g (5½ oz/1 cup) plain (all-purpose) flour
2 large free-range eggs
125 ml (4 fl oz/½ cup) milk
170 g (6 oz/3 cups) flaked coconut
20 large raw king prawns (shrimp), peeled and deveined, leaving the tails intact
peanut oil, for deep-frying
1 bunch (90 g/3¼ oz) coriander (cilantro); reserve the roots for the dipping sauce below
lime or lemon wedges, to serve

SWEET CHILLI & GINGER DIPPING SAUCE

500 g (1 lb 2 oz) long red chillies, roughly chopped
4 garlic cloves, roughly chopped
1 thumb-sized piece of fresh ginger, peeled and roughly chopped
coriander (cilantro) roots (reserved from the bunch above), washed well
625 ml (21½ fl oz/2½ cups) white vinegar
550 g (1 lb 4 oz/2½ cups) sugar
1 teaspoon fine sea salt

Add the flour to a bowl and season with sea salt and freshly ground black pepper. In a separate bowl, whisk together the eggs and milk. Put the coconut in a third bowl. Take the prawns, one at a time, and dip them in the flour, then the egg mixture, and lastly the coconut, making sure you get a really good covering of coconut onto the prawn. Lay the prawns on a flat tray and set aside, or cover and refrigerate until required. (This step can be done a few hours ahead, or even the day before.)

To make the dipping sauce, place the chilli, garlic, ginger and reserved coriander roots in a food processor. Add the vinegar and process until smooth. Pour the mixture into a heavy-based saucepan and place over low heat. Add the sugar and salt, then cook, stirring, for a minute or two until the sugar has dissolved. Increase the heat and bring to the boil, then reduce the heat and simmer for about 20 minutes, or until the sauce has reduced and thickened; adjust the seasoning. (The dipping sauce can also be made several hours or a day ahead.)

Just before serving, pour about 10 cm (4 inches) peanut oil into a large heavy-based saucepan and heat to 180°C (350°F), or until a cube of bread dropped into the oil turns golden in 15 seconds.

Cook five prawns at a time, for about 3 minutes each batch, taking care to bring the oil back up to the right temperature between each batch. Watch the oil doesn't get too hot: you want the prawns to be cooked through, and the coconut nicely golden and crunchy-looking.

Drain on paper towel and serve immediately, garnished with coriander, with the dipping sauce and lime or lemon wedges for squeezing over.

We like to serve these delicate little dumplings on Chinese spoons, with a drizzle of the dipping sauce. They are also lovely served from a bamboo steamer at home, as part of a Chinese banquet.

STEAMED PRAWN & GINGER DUMPLINGS WITH DIPPING SAUCE

MAKES **20**
PREPARATION **30 MINUTES**   COOKING **20 MINUTES**

20 round won ton wrappers
½ bunch (45 g/1½ oz) coriander
   (cilantro), leaves picked
vegetable oil spray

MALT VINEGAR, SOY & GINGER DIPPING SAUCE

2 tablespoons grated or very finely
   chopped fresh ginger
2 tablespoons light soy sauce
2 tablespoons malt vinegar
1 teaspoon sugar
½ teaspoon sesame oil
1 small red chilli, finely chopped

FILLING

400 g (14 oz) raw king prawns (shrimp),
   peeled and deveined
2 spring onions (scallions), finely
   chopped
1 teaspoon grated or very finely chopped
   fresh ginger
1 teaspoon oyster sauce
½ teaspoon soy sauce
½ teaspoon sesame oil
1 teaspoon cornflour (cornstarch)
¼ teaspoon ground white pepper
1 egg white

The closer the dumplings are prepared to serving time, the better, so it's a good idea to have everything organised and ready to go.

Combine the dipping sauce ingredients in a small bowl, stirring to dissolve the sugar; set aside. Place all the filling ingredients in a food processor and whiz briefly to a roughly chopped consistency.

Lay your won ton wrappers on a clean surface. Brush the edges with a little water and put a coriander sprig on the bottom half, closest to you. Place a heaped teaspoon of the filling on each one. Fold the won ton wrapper over, so you have a half-moon shape, then press the edges together; you can make nice little pleats along the edge if you want to make the dumplings really pretty.

Line a bamboo or metal steamer with baking paper, then spray with vegetable oil spray. Make a few holes in the baking paper with a sharp knife. Set the steamer over a saucepan of simmering water, ensuring the steamer doesn't touch the water. Working in batches, place some dumplings in the steamer, being careful not to overcrowd it, then put the lid on and steam for 5 minutes.

Serve the warm dumplings on Chinese spoons with a drizzle of the dipping sauce, or straight from the steamer basket, with a small bowl of the dipping sauce on the side.

BABY LAMB & HARISSA SAUSAGE ROLLS WITH EGGPLANT PICKLE

MAKES **36**
PREPARATION **1 HOUR**   COOKING **35 MINUTES**

HARISSA

10 large dried red chillies
1 teaspoon coriander seeds
1 teaspoon caraway seeds
2 tablespoons olive oil
1 brown onion, chopped
1 red capsicum (pepper), chopped
4 garlic cloves, chopped
1 teaspoon sea salt
1 teaspoon ground cumin

FILLING

1 kg (2 lb 4 oz) minced (ground) lamb
250 ml (9 fl oz/1 cup) milk
125 g (4½ oz/2 cups) fresh sourdough
    breadcrumbs
100 g (3½ oz/⅔ cup) currants
40 g (1½ oz/¼ cup) pine nuts, toasted
2 tablespoons Harissa (see above)
2 garlic cloves, crushed
2 tablespoons finely chopped mint
2 tablespoons finely chopped coriander
    (cilantro) leaves and stalks
2 teaspoons sea salt
½ teaspoon ground white pepper

FOR THE HARISSA

Soak the dried chillies in a bowl of hot water for 30 minutes. Drain, then remove the seeds and stems.

In a dry frying pan over medium heat, toast the coriander seeds and caraway seeds for 5 minutes, until fragrant.

Tip the toasted seeds into a heavy-based saucepan. Add the soaked chillies and remaining harissa ingredients and cook over medium heat for 30 minutes, stirring regularly to ensure the mixture doesn't stick to the bottom of the pan.

Allow to cool, then blend to a smooth consistency using a food processor or hand-held stick blender. Transfer to an airtight container and refrigerate until required; the harissa will keep for up to 1 month in the fridge, if you handle it well, by always using a clean spoon when dipping into it.

FOR THE FILLING

Place all the filling ingredients in a bowl. Using your hands, mix for about 5 minutes, to work the proteins of the meat and combine all the flavours. (If you have time, you could cover the filling and rest it in the fridge for 1 hour, or even overnight.)

TO MAKE AND BAKE THE ROLLS

Preheat the oven to 180°C (350°F). In a small bowl, whisk together the egg and milk using a fork, to make an egg wash.

Divide the puff pastry into two even portions. On a lightly floured workbench, roll out one piece of pastry into a large rectangle, measuring about 85 cm x 20 cm (33½ inches x 8 inches), and about 5 mm (¼ inch) thick.

Divide the lamb filling into two even portions. Lay half the mixture along the middle of the pastry rectangle, shaping it into a log. Use a pastry brush to brush the egg wash down the long side of the pastry, close to the lamb mixture. Fold the pastry over the top of the filling, then press the pastry pieces together, overlapping them. Trim the excess pastry.

Repeat with the remaining pastry and lamb mixture, to make another long sausage roll. Brush the rolls with the remaining egg wash, then sprinkle with the sesame seeds.

Cut each roll into 18 small cocktail-sized pieces, giving you 36 mini sausage rolls. Place on two baking trays lined with baking paper, then bake for 30 minutes, or until the pastry is golden brown.

Serve warm, with the eggplant pickle.

TO FINISH THE ROLLS

1 free-range egg
60 ml (2 fl oz/¼ cup) milk
1 quantity Easy rough puff pastry
    (Toolbox, page 35)
2 tablespoons white sesame seeds
Eggplant pickle (Toolbox, page 24),
    to serve

SMOKED SALMON ROULADE WITH SOUR CREAM & SALMON PEARLS

MAKES **60 PIECES**
PREPARATION **1¼ HOURS + 20 MINUTES RESTING** COOKING **30 MINUTES**

150 g (5½ oz/1 cup) plain
   (all-purpose) flour
pinch of sea salt
1 large free-range egg
500 ml (17 fl oz/2 cups) milk
2 tablespoons butter, melted
vegetable oil spray
150 g (5½ oz) sour cream
30 slices smoked salmon, about 750 g
   (1 lb 10 oz) in total
4 tablespoons finely chopped chives
100 g (3½ oz) jar of salmon roe
thin lemon wedges, to serve

Place a heavy mixing bowl on a damp, folded tea towel. Sift the flour and salt into the bowl, then make a well in the centre. Whisk together the egg, milk and butter, then pour into the flour well. Gently mix, slowly pulling at the wall of flour and incorporating it into the liquid until you have a smooth batter. Cover and rest for 20 minutes.

Place a 22 cm (8½ inch) crepe pan over medium heat and spray with a little vegetable oil spray. Ladle the smallest amount of batter into the pan, to get a very thin crepe. Gently swirl the pan so the batter is even and runs out to the edge. Cook for 1 minute, or until little bubbles form and the sides start to pull away from the pan. Using a spatula, gently flip the crepe over. Cook for 1–2 minutes, or until the batter has set, then slide onto a plate. Cook the remaining batter in the same way, oiling the pan each time, and stacking the crepes on top of each other. They can be left to cool and covered with plastic wrap for a few hours, but it is best to make up the roulades while the crepes are fresh.

To assemble the roulades, lay the crepes on your workbench and smear each one with a tablespoon of sour cream. On each crepe, lay three slices of smoked salmon, covering as much of the crepe as possible. Sprinkle with the chives, season generously, then roll up tightly. Now, this is the important bit: lay a 25 cm (10 inch) square of plastic wrap on the bench. Place one roulade in the centre, near the bottom, and roll up. Twist one end of the plastic very tightly and tie in a knot, then do the same with the other end, to form a very tight little log shape. Continue with the remaining roulades, then refrigerate until needed.

To serve, remove the plastic from each roulade, trim the ends off, then cut each into six pieces. Top each piece with a little dollop of sour cream and salmon roe. Serve with dainty lemon wedges.

ROSEMARY & GARLIC TOASTS WITH SMOKED TROUT OR GOAT'S CHEESE

MAKES **24–30 TOASTS**
PREPARATION **30 MINUTES**   BAKING **10 MINUTES**

ROSEMARY & GARLIC TOASTS

1 sourdough batard
olive oil, for drizzling
4 rosemary sprigs, leaves chopped
4 garlic cloves, finely chopped

SMOKED TROUT & HORSERADISH CREAM

1 smoked river trout, weighing about
   200 g (7 oz)
4 tablespoons sour cream
2 tablespoons bottled horseradish
1 teaspoon dijon mustard
thyme sprigs or chopped chives,
   to garnish
thin lemon zest strips, to garnish

GOAT'S CHEESE, RED CAPSICUM JAM & BASIL

180 g (6 oz) soft goat's cheese
3 tablespoons Red capsicum jam
   (Toolbox, page 25)
½ bunch (60 g/2¼ oz) basil, leaves
   picked and roughly chopped

FOR THE ROSEMARY & GARLIC TOASTS

Preheat the oven to 180°C (350°F). Line a large baking tray with baking paper.

Cut the bread into thin slices, about 5 mm (¼ inch) thick, then cut each slice into four pieces. Spread the slices on the baking tray. Drizzle very generously with olive oil, then sprinkle with the rosemary and garlic. Season with sea salt and freshly ground black pepper.

Bake for 10 minutes, or until golden and crunchy. Remove from the oven and leave to cool, then store in an airtight container until required; they will keep fresh for up to 1 week.

TO ASSEMBLE

Lay the rosemary and garlic toasts out on your workbench.

For the smoked trout topping, take the skin and head off the trout, and remove all the bones. Place the flesh in a bowl and check again for any very small bones. In a separate bowl, mix together the sour cream, horseradish and mustard, then adjust the seasoning. Top all or half of the toasts with the horseradish cream and a few lovely, velvety, smoky pieces of trout. Garnish with thyme or chives and lemon zest strips.

For the goat's cheese topping, simply smear half or all the toasts with the goat's cheese, add a small dollop of capsicum jam, then garnish with the basil.

Arrange your toasts on a platter, sprinkle with sea salt and freshly ground black pepper and serve.

Vonnie is a family friend, and this recipe belonged to her dad, Mr Gow. For the first decade of my Balmain store, he would deliver these dim sum to me, frozen in bags of 50. Sadly, Mr Gow is no longer with us, but we make these every Friday in his memory. There are lots of ground rules here, as with most recipes that have been lovingly handed down through the years, so follow carefully and respectfully, as we have done. RIP Mr Gow.

PORK & WATER CHESTNUT DIM SUM WITH SOY DIPPER

MAKES **ABOUT 60**
PREPARATION **40 MINUTES + SEVERAL HOURS CHILLING**   COOKING **50 MINUTES**

250 g (9 oz) packet of square egg won ton wrappers
vegetable oil spray

FOR THE FILLING
500 g (1 lb 2 oz) finely minced (ground) pork, preferably from the sow
500 g (1 lb 2 oz) coarsely minced (ground) pork, preferably from the sow
150 g (5½ oz) tin water chestnuts, drained and finely chopped
1 free-range egg
1 tablespoon toasted sesame seeds
1 spring onion (scallion), finely chopped
1½ tablespoons caster (superfine) sugar
1 teaspoon fine sea salt
1 teaspoon light soy sauce (Pearl brand)
1 teaspoon oyster sauce (Lee Kum Kee)
1 tablespoon cornflour (cornstarch)
½ teaspoon ground white pepper
1 tablespoon chicken powder (Knorr brand)

SOY DIPPER
2 tablespoons light soy sauce
½ teaspoon oyster sauce
a few drops of sesame oil
¼ small red chilli, chopped

Place all the filling ingredients in a large bowl and mix until well combined. Cover and set aside in the fridge for an hour or two, or overnight if preferred, to let the flavours combine.

Line a large tray with baking paper and lightly spray with vegetable oil spray. Combine all the soy dipper ingredients in a small bowl.

Place a large saucepan, which will fit a steamer basket on the top, over high heat and fill with hot water. Line a steamer basket with baking paper and spray the paper with oil. Make a few holes in the baking paper with a sharp knife.

Lay 10 won ton wrappers on a clean workbench. Place a tablespoon (about 20 g/¾ oz) of the pork mixture on each one. Gather the won ton wrapper up around the filling and give it a good squeeze, leaving a bit of the filling showing at the top. Continue using up all the won ton wrappers and pork mixture.

Place a batch of dim sum in the steamer, taking care not to overcrowd the steamer. Put the lid on and steam for 10–12 minutes, or until the pork is cooked all the way through.

Serve warm, with the soy dipper.

TIP: It is best to steam these dumplings close to the time of assembly. However, once steamed, they will keep, well covered in the fridge, for several days. Simply reheat them in the microwave with a dash of water, covered with plastic wrap, until completely heated through.

I love an elegant finger sandwich. Quite often, early in the morning in the Simmone Logue kitchen, all you can hear is the gentle hum of electric knives, cutting and trimming the many sandwich fingers for serving later that day.

DAINTY SMOKED SALMON & CREAM CHEESE FINGER SANDWICHES

MAKES **24 FINGER SANDWICHES**
PREPARATION **30 MINUTES**

115 g (4 oz/¾ cup) currants, soaked in hot water for 30 minutes

4 tablespoons chopped pickled ginger, drained

440 g (15½ oz) cream cheese, at room temperature

300 g (10½ oz) smoked salmon, sliced into thin strips

4 tablespoons chopped dill

4 tablespoons chopped chives

2 super-fresh loaves of sliced white toasting bread; you'll need 24 slices

In a bowl, combine the currants, ginger, cream cheese, smoked salmon, dill and chives. Mix gently, then season to taste with sea salt and freshly ground black pepper.

Have a large, clean damp tea towel at the ready, to keep your dainty sandwiches as fresh as possible.

Lay 12 bread slices down on your workbench and spread 2 tablespoons of the salmon mixture on each. Top each with another slice of bread. As you assemble each sandwich, cover it with the damp tea towel — trust me, if there is any sign of a breeze coming through your kitchen, your lovely fresh sandwiches will dry out.

Using an electric knife, cut the crusts off each sandwich, then cut each sandwich into two fingers. Keep the sandwich fingers covered with the damp tea towel until you are ready to plate them.

> *These are so yummy, it's hard to stop at one. Being a little more substantial than many cocktail food items, they're also great for filling up your guests. If 48 pies is too much for one occasion, you can simply freeze half the duck filling for next time.*

LITTLE RED THAI DUCK PIES

MAKES **48**
PREPARATION **40 MINUTES**   COOKING **1 HOUR 40 MINUTES**

1 free-range duck, about 2 kg (4 lb 8 oz)

4 star anise

1 thumb-sized piece of fresh ginger, sliced

1 brown onion, roughly chopped

6 tablespoons good-quality red curry paste

2 tablespoons olive oil

375 ml (13 fl oz/1½ cups) coconut milk

4 kaffir lime leaves

1 tablespoon caster (superfine) sugar

1 tablespoon fish sauce

½ teaspoon sea salt

3 spring onions (scallions), finely chopped

4 tablespoons roughly chopped coriander (cilantro) leaves

vegetable oil spray

2 quantities Sour cream pastry (Toolbox, page 34)

1 free-range egg, beaten with 60 ml (2 fl oz/¼ cup) milk to make an egg wash

Preheat the oven to 160°C (315°F). Line a baking dish with baking paper. Place the duck in the baking dish. Open the cavity of the bird and place the star anise, ginger and onion inside. Smear 2 tablespoons of the curry paste over the bird and massage it in. Pour 250 ml (9 fl oz/ 1 cup) water into the baking dish, then cover tightly with baking paper and a sheet of foil. Transfer to the oven and roast for 1 hour. Remove from the oven and leave until cool enough to handle. Strip the meat off the duck, chop it into small pieces and set aside.

Place a large heavy-based saucepan over medium heat. Add the olive oil and remaining curry paste. Cook the paste for 5 minutes, or until the oil has split out and it is lovely and fragrant. Stir in the coconut milk, add the lime leaves and cook gently for 10 minutes. Stir in the sugar, fish sauce and salt. Add the chopped duck, spring onion and coriander and cook for a further 5 minutes, or until the duck is heated through. Place in a container, cover and refrigerate until ready to use; if making only 24 pies, freeze half the duck filling for your next lot of pies.

When ready to bake the pies, preheat the oven to 180°C (350°F). Lightly spray 48 tart tins, each 6 cm (2½ inches) in size, with vegetable oil spray. On a lightly floured workbench, roll out the pastry to about 5 mm (¼ inch) thick. Using an 8 cm (3¼ inch) cookie cutter, cut out 48 pastry rounds, then gently push them into the tart tins. Spoon a heaped tablespoon (about 55 g/2 oz) of the duck mixture into each pastry case.

Gather up the left-over pastry and roll it out again. Using a smaller cookie cutter, say about 6.5 cm (2½ inches), cut another 48 circles for the tops. Press the pastry tops onto the pies and brush with egg wash. (Any left-over filling and pastry can be frozen for another time.) Prick the tops with a fork to let the steam out. Bake the tarts for 12 minutes, or until the pastry is golden. Serve warm.

Chapter Nine

SWEETS, TARTS, PUDDINGS & KISSES

THIS CHAPTER IS FOR ALL THE DESSERT-HEADS OUT THERE, WHO OVER THE YEARS HAVE PLEADED WITH ME FOR THE RECIPES OF THESE SHINING BEAUTIES.

I particularly love the Baked lemon tart (page 198), Pavlova with sweet labneh and poached cherries (page 201), and the old-fashioned Vanilla slice (page 189). Other sentimental favourites such as the Apple pie (page 206) and Pumpkin pie (page 202) take me right back to my childhood, when my Pa would bake them for us on Sundays...

I hope that in this chapter you'll find a few new sweet treasures to relish with those you love.

These are just so good, and not too big, so you don't feel guilty when you indulge in one — although it's very hard to stop at just one! These caramel kisses freeze brilliantly in an airtight container, so you can make up a huge batch by doubling or tripling the recipe, and getting the kids to help press the biscuit mixture into your mini muffin tins. I like to give them as gifts to my friends and family, who find them irresistible.

CARAMEL KISSES

MAKES **36**
PREPARATION **40 MINUTES**   COOKING **30 MINUTES**

vegetable oil spray

BISCUIT BASE
200 g (7 oz) digestive biscuits (cookies)
40 g (1½ oz/scant ½ cup) desiccated
   coconut
30 g (1 oz) light brown sugar
50 g (1¾ oz/⅓ cup) plain (all-purpose)
   flour
80 g (2¾ oz) unsalted butter, melted
80 ml (2¾ fl oz/⅓ cup) golden syrup or
   treacle
1 tablespoon milk

CARAMEL FILLING
400 g (14 oz) tin condensed milk
50 g (1¾ oz) unsalted butter
50 ml (1¾ fl oz) golden syrup or treacle

CHOCOLATE GANACHE TOPPING
100 ml (3½ fl oz) thin (pouring/
   whipping) cream
100 g (3½ oz) good-quality dark
   chocolate, chopped

Preheat the oven to 170°C (325°F). Lightly spray three 12-hole mini muffin tins with vegetable oil spray.

To make the biscuit base, use a food processor or blender to whiz the biscuits into fine crumbs. Tip the crumbs into a bowl, add the coconut, sugar and flour and mix together. Pour in the melted butter, golden syrup and milk and mix until combined.

Take a heaped teaspoon of the mixture and roll it into a small ball, then press it into one of the muffin holes, and all the way up the side, as if you were making a little clay 'pinch pot'. Repeat with the remaining biscuit mixture.

Combine the caramel filling ingredients in a saucepan. Stir over low heat for about 5 minutes, or until the mixture starts to thicken. Pour the caramel into a jug with a good spout, then three-quarters fill the biscuit cases with the caramel, leaving room for the topping.

Transfer to the oven and bake for 20 minutes, then remove from the oven and leave to cool completely.

To make the topping, heat the cream in a small saucepan until it is quite hot. Whisk in the chocolate until the ganache is nice and thick, and all the chocolate has melted. Pour the ganache into a small jug, then pour this shiny chocolate topping onto your little caramel kisses.

Place the caramel kisses in the refrigerator to set; they will keep in an airtight container in the fridge for up to 1 week.

VANILLA SLICE WITH PASSIONFRUIT ICING

MAKES 12 SLICES
PREPARATION 30 MINUTES + 6 HOURS CHILLING   COOKING 45 MINUTES

½ quantity Easy rough puff pastry (Toolbox, page 35)
passionfruit pulp, for drizzling

CUSTARD
500 ml (17 fl oz/2 cups) milk
250 ml (9 fl oz/1 cup) thin (pouring/whipping) cream
50 g (1¾ oz) unsalted butter, chopped
110 g (3¾ oz/½ cup) caster (superfine) sugar
2 teaspoons vanilla extract
40 g (1½ oz/⅓ cup) cornflour (cornstarch), mixed to a smooth slurry with 125 ml (4 fl oz/½ cup) water
6 free-range egg yolks

PASSIONFRUIT ICING
250 g (9 oz/2 cups) icing (confectioners') sugar
100 g (3½ oz) butter, softened
4 tablespoons passionfruit pulp
juice of ½ lemon

Line two 38 cm x 26 cm (15 inch x 10½ inch) baking trays with baking paper. On a lightly floured workbench, roll out half the pastry to about 5 mm (¼ inch) thick, to the size of the baking trays, then place on one of the trays. Roll out the other pastry portion, placing it on the other tray. Dock each pastry sheet with a fork, then top each with a sheet of baking paper, then another tray of some sort. Rest in the fridge for 20 minutes; meanwhile, preheat the oven to 180°C (350°F).

Bake the rested pastry sheets for 30 minutes. Remove from the oven to cool completely, then trim each to a 20 cm (8 inch) square.

To make the custard, put the milk, cream, butter, sugar and vanilla in a saucepan. Bring to the boil, then remove from the heat. Using a hand whisk, mix in the cornflour slurry and egg yolks. Place back over medium heat and whisk for a few minutes, until thickened into a custard.

Line a 20 cm (8 inch) square cake tin with baking paper, letting it overhang the sides of the tin, to make it easier to lift the slice out. Line the base of the tin with a puff pastry portion. Pour the custard over. Top with the second piece of pastry and very gently push it down.

To make the icing, sift the icing sugar into a bowl, add the butter and beat until light and creamy. Mix in the passionfruit pulp and lemon juice until combined, then spread the icing over the top of the slice. Cover and chill for 6 hours, or preferably overnight, to set the custard.

To serve, lift the slice out of the tin, using the baking paper to help you. Using a sharp knife, cut into 12 pieces and drizzle with extra passionfruit pulp. Any leftover vanilla slice will keep for a few days in an airtight container in the fridge.

The great thing about éclairs — besides their pure deliciousness! — is that you can make the choux pastry and bake the éclair shells ahead, then freeze them to be filled at a later date. In this version, we're piping crème pâtissière inside the éclairs and dipping them in chocolate ganache... but you can fill these lovely light and wondrous éclairs with all sorts of luscious things, so let your imagination go crazy.

CHOCOLATE ÉCLAIRS

MAKES **30**
PREPARATION **1 HOUR**   COOKING **45 MINUTES**

CHOUX PASTRY
100 g (3½ oz) unsalted butter
150 g (5½ oz/1 cup) plain (all-purpose)
  flour
1 teaspoon sugar
¼ teaspoon sea salt
4 free-range eggs

FOR THE CHOUX PASTRY
Preheat the oven to 200°C (400°F). Line two large flat baking trays with baking paper.

In a saucepan, bring the butter and 250 ml (9 fl oz/1 cup) water to the boil. Using a wooden spoon, stir in the flour, sugar and salt. Keep stirring over medium heat for about 10 minutes, or until the raw flour taste has cooked out.

Scoop the batter into a bowl. Using an electric mixer fitted with a paddle attachment, beat until cool. Add the eggs, one at a time, beating well between each addition.

Spoon the batter into a piping (icing) bag fitted with a 1.5–2 cm (⅝–¾ inch) star nozzle. In little straight lines, about 7 cm (2¾ inches) long, pipe 30 pastry portions onto the baking trays, allowing room for slight spreading.

Transfer to the oven and bake, without opening the door again, for 20 minutes, or until the pastry is golden brown. It's important not to open the door of the oven until the last few minutes of baking, as it's the steam that is created in the oven that gives the pastry its lift.

Remove the éclairs from the oven and leave to cool, then store in an airtight container until required. They will keep in the pantry for 1 week, or in the freezer for 3 months. (If they've been frozen, thaw them out, then refresh in a 150°C/300°F oven for 5 minutes before filling.)

FOR THE CRÈME PÂTISSIÈRE

Put the cream, milk and vanilla bean in a heavy-based saucepan and bring to a simmer over medium heat.

Place the sugar, egg and three egg yolks in a bowl. Using an electric mixer, whisk until pale and creamy. In three batches, sift the flour and cornflour into the mixture, whisking until combined.

When the milk is at boiling point, add half to the egg mixture, stirring constantly, then pour in the remainder, whisking again. Remove the vanilla bean, then pour the egg mixture back into the saucepan and simmer for 2 minutes, whisking until smooth.

Pour into a bowl, place a piece of plastic wrap directly on the surface so a skin doesn't form, then chill until required. The crème pâtissière will last for a good week in the fridge.

TO ASSEMBLE THE ÉCLAIRS

Whip the cream to stiff peaks, using an electric mixer. Cut the éclairs in half lengthways, all the way through. Using a piping (icing) bag, pipe some crème pâtissière onto the bottom half of each éclair, then pipe the whipped cream over the crème pâtissière.

Dip the other half of the éclairs into the chocolate ganache and place on top of the whipped cream. Sprinkle with the pistachios. Once assembled, the éclairs are best enjoyed within a few hours.

CRÈME PÂTISSIÈRE

150 ml (5 fl oz) thin (pouring/whipping) cream
350 ml (12 fl oz) full-cream milk
1 vanilla bean, split in half
75 g (2½ oz/⅓ cup) caster (superfine) sugar
1 free-range egg, plus 3 free-range egg yolks
2 tablespoons plain (all-purpose) flour
2 tablespoons cornflour (cornstarch)

TO ASSEMBLE

600 ml (21 fl oz) thin (pouring/whipping) cream
1 quantity Chocolate ganache (page 205)
150 g (5½ oz/1 cup) pistachio nuts, toasted and crushed

I love autumn, when quinces are at their best. I spend days out on the farm, foraging and gathering up gnarly, sweet-perfumed fruit to bring back to our stores. We make quince paste, slow braise them in our Moroccan lamb dishes, and top our frangipane tarts with them — but by far my favourite way to use quince is to poach it and arrange elegant little slices on top of these tarts. The colour and perfume of poached quince just blows me away. There must be a God in heaven!

CRÈME PÂTISSIÈRE TARTS WITH POACHED QUINCE

MAKES **24 COCKTAIL-SIZED TARTS**
PREPARATION **1 HOUR**   COOKING **1¾ HOURS + 15 MINUTES BAKING**

1 quantity Sweet almond shortcrust
  pastry (Toolbox, page 37)
1 quantity Crème pâtissière (page 191)

POACHED QUINCE
6 quinces
zest and juice of 1 lemon
220 g (7¾ oz/1 cup) sugar
2 vanilla beans, cut in half lengthways
3 fresh bay leaves

Preheat the oven to 180°C (350°F). On a lightly floured workbench, roll out the pastry to about 5 mm (¼ inch) thick.

Using an 8 cm (3¼ inch) cookie cutter, cut out 24 pastry circles, and use them to line 24 individual 7 cm (2¾ inch) mini flan (tart) tins. Bake for 10–12 minutes, or until the pastry is golden. Remove from the oven and leave to cool, then store in an airtight container until required.

To poach the quinces, peel them, cut them in half, then remove the cores. Slice into wedges, place in a bowl with a squeeze of lemon, and gently toss. In a heavy-based saucepan, combine the sugar, vanilla beans, bay leaves and 750 ml (26 fl oz/3 cups) water. Bring to the boil, stirring to dissolve the sugar. Add the quince and top with a piece of baking paper, then cook at a low simmer for 1½ hours, or until the quince is tender.

Using a slotted spoon, remove all the quince pieces to an airtight container, then keep reducing the poaching liquid at a rapid bubble for 10–15 minutes, until it has reduced by about half, and you have a lovely sticky, viscose syrup. Pour the syrup over the quince, then seal. It will keep for several weeks in the fridge.

To assemble the tarts, spoon a little crème pâtissière into the tart cases. Cut the quince into elegant slices and arrange over the top. Drizzle with a little quince poaching syrup and serve.

> *Besides being terribly moreish, the beauty of these little cocktail-sized bombs of deliciousness is that you can make the doughnut batter a day ahead, and fry them up just before you pass them around, piping hot. We often serve these at the end of a function; guests are always asking for the recipe.*

ITALIAN RICOTTA DOUGHNUTS WITH CHOCOLATE BRANDY SAUCE

MAKES **ABOUT 24**
PREPARATION **30 MINUTES + AT LEAST 1 HOUR RESTING**   COOKING **30 MINUTES**

125 g (4½ oz) unsalted butter, softened
160 g (5½ oz/¾ cup) caster (superfine) sugar
4 free-range eggs
150 g (5½ oz/1 cup) plain (all-purpose) flour
zest of 1 lemon
zest of 1 orange
700 g (1 lb 9 oz/3 cups) ricotta cheese
peanut oil, for deep-frying

CINNAMON SUGAR
100 g (3½ oz) caster (superfine) sugar
1 tablespoon ground cinnamon

CHOCOLATE BRANDY SAUCE
125 g (4½ oz) best-quality chocolate
125 ml (4½ fl oz) thin (pouring/ whipping) cream
2 tablespoons brandy

Using an electric mixer, beat the butter and sugar together until pale and creamy. Add the eggs one at a time. Add the flour and all the citrus zest and beat until you have a smooth batter. Fold the ricotta through, then cover and rest in the refrigerator for 1 hour, or overnight.

In a large saucepan, heat the oil to 160°C (315°F), or until a cube of bread dropped into the oil turns golden brown in 30–35 seconds. You don't want the oil too hot, as the doughnuts need to cook all the way through to the inside.

For each doughnut, dollop a heaped tablespoon of the batter into the oil. Fry the doughnuts in batches of about four or five, for at least 4 minutes each time, or until they are golden and cooked through, rolling them around in the oil using metal tongs so they colour evenly. Drain on paper towel and keep warm while cooking the remaining doughnuts.

Meanwhile, combine the cinnamon sugar ingredients in a small bowl. Place all the chocolate brandy sauce ingredients in a saucepan and stir over medium–low heat for 2–3 minutes, until the chocolate has melted and the sauce is smooth and hot. Pour into a heatproof dipping bowl.

Serve the doughnuts warm, sprinkled with the cinnamon sugar, with the chocolate brandy sauce on the side.

TIP: For an alternative sauce, you could make a gorgeous raspberry coulis by blending 125 g (4½ oz/1 cup) raspberries with the juice of 1 lime and 75 g (2½ oz/⅓ cup) caster (superfine) sugar.

BREAD & BUTTER PUDDING WITH SAUTERNES & PEARS

SERVES **8**
PREPARATION **30 MINUTES + 1 HOUR RESTING**
COOKING **1 HOUR**

125 g (4½ oz) unsalted butter, softened, plus extra for greasing

1 day-old sourdough batard, or a loaf of your favourite left-over bread, the ends sliced off, and the rest of the loaf cut into about 12 slices the thickness of your finger

vanilla bean ice cream, to serve

SAUTERNES-POACHED PEARS

375 ml (13 fl oz/1½ cups) Sauternes

110 g (3¾ oz/½ cup) sugar

1 vanilla bean, split in half

8 pears, stems on; I use corella pears as they are visually beautiful, but any variety will do

CUSTARD

9 large free-range eggs

1½ teaspoons ground nutmeg

1 teaspoon vanilla extract

295 g (10¼ oz/1⅓ cups) caster (superfine) sugar

330 ml (11¼ fl oz/1⅓ cups) thin (pouring/ whipping) cream

330 ml (11¼ fl oz/1⅓ cups) full-cream milk

To poach the pears, combine the Sauternes, sugar, vanilla bean and 250 ml (9 fl oz/1 cup) water in a heavy-based pan. Bring to a simmer. Add the pears, adding a little more water if needed to fully submerge them. Simmer gently for 15 minutes, or until the pears can be pierced with a skewer. Remove the pears from the pan. Keep cooking the liquid at a rapid bubble for 10–15 minutes, or until reduced to a lovely sticky, viscose syrup. Place the pears back in the syrup until ready to serve.

To make the custard, put the eggs, nutmeg and vanilla in a bowl. Add half the sugar and whisk together with a hand whisk. Add the cream and milk and whisk again until combined.

Butter a shallow 28 cm x 20 cm (11¼ inch x 8 inch) baking dish. Butter each slice of bread, then place a layer of bread in the baking dish; you may need to cut a slice or two so they fit well. Don't overlap the slices, or the custard won't soak into the bread. Ladle a layer of custard over the top. Add another layer of buttered bread, then more custard, until you have used all the bread and custard. Push the bread down under the custard, then cover and leave to rest for 1 hour.

Preheat the oven to 150°C (300°F). Find a baking dish that is larger than the one you've made your pudding in. Place the smaller baking dish inside the larger one, then pour enough hot water into the larger baking dish to come halfway up the side of your pudding. (This will create a bain-marie, to help the pudding bake slowly and stop the custard curdling.) Carefully transfer the baking dishes to the oven. Bake for 30 minutes, or until the custard doesn't run when the pudding is gently pushed in the middle. Serve warm, with a scoop of ice cream, the poached pears and a drizzle of the poaching syrup.

BAKED LEMON TART

MAKES **1 X 23 CM (9 INCH) TART**: SERVES **10**
PREPARATION **30 MINUTES**   BAKING **50 MINUTES**

1 quantity Sweet almond shortcrust pastry (Toolbox, page 37), chilled in the fridge for 30 minutes before using
thick (double/heavy) cream, to serve
icing (confectioners') sugar, for dusting

FOR THE FILLING
5 free-range eggs
220 g (7¾ oz/1 cup) caster (superfine) sugar
300 ml (10½ fl oz) thick (double/heavy) cream
zest and juice of 2 lemons

Grease a 23 cm (9 inch) loose-based fluted flan (tart) tin. On a lightly floured workbench, roll out the pastry to about 8 mm (⅜ inch) thick, then use it to line the flan tin. Trim the edges, then leave to rest in the fridge for 20 minutes. Meanwhile, preheat the oven to 180°C (350°F).

Place the flan tin on a baking tray. Line the tart shell with baking paper and fill with baking beads or uncooked rice or dried beans. Blind bake the pastry for 10 minutes, then remove the baking beads or rice and bake for a further 10 minutes. Remove from the oven and leave to cool slightly. Turn the oven temperature down to 160°C (315°F).

Place all the filling ingredients in a bowl. Whisk using an electric mixer until smooth and well combined. Set aside to rest for 10 minutes.

Pour the filling into the tart shell. Bake for 30 minutes, or until the filling has set. Remove from the oven and leave to cool to room temperature. (If making the tart ahead, you can refrigerate it and bring it back to room temperature for serving.)

Serve with thick cream and a dusting of icing sugar.

To me, this is a real 'adults only' kind of dessert; I use it a lot at home for special occasions. Accompanied by a generous dollop of thick cream, it's heavenly. It's important to let the prunes really soak up the Armagnac and to not overcook the frangipane, as it should be lovely and moist.

PRUNE, FRANGIPANE & ARMAGNAC TART WITH DOUBLE CREAM

MAKES **1 X 23 CM (9 INCH) TART**; SERVES **8**
PREPARATION **40 MINUTES + 20 MINUTES RESTING**
COOKING **15 MINUTES + 50 MINUTES BAKING**

1 quantity Sweet almond shortcrust pastry (Toolbox, page 37)
150 ml (5 fl oz) Armagnac or Cognac
200 g (7 oz/1 cup) pitted prunes
1½ quantities Frangipane (Toolbox, page 45)
icing (confectioners') sugar, for dusting
300 ml (10½ fl oz) thick (double/heavy) cream, to serve

Grease a 23 cm (9 inch) loose-based fluted flan (tart) tin; make sure the tin is at least 10 cm (4 inches) deep. On a lightly floured workbench, roll out the pastry to about 8 mm (⅜ inch) thick, then ease it into the flan tin. Press the pastry into the tin and trim the edges. Rest in the fridge for 20 minutes. Meanwhile, preheat the oven to 180°C (350°F).

Line the tart shell with baking paper and fill with baking beads or uncooked rice or dried beans. Blind bake the pastry for 10 minutes, then remove the baking beads or rice and bake for a further 10 minutes. Remove from the oven and leave to cool slightly. Turn the oven temperature down to 160°C (315°F).

Meanwhile, warm the Armagnac in a small saucepan over low heat. Add the prunes and leave to simmer for about 10 minutes, to allow the prunes to soak up all the goodness. Set aside.

Spoon the frangipane into the baked tart shell, using a spatula to smooth the top. Dot the prunes over the tart and bake for 30 minutes, or until the frangipane is set.

Remove from the oven and leave to cool. Dust with icing sugar and serve with thick cream. Any leftovers will keep for a few days in the fridge.

> *Who doesn't love a pavlova? If you live in the southern hemisphere, try serving this particularly decadent version around Christmas time, when cherries are at their best and you're looking for a festive dessert to impress.*

BABY PAVLOVAS WITH SWEET LABNEH & POACHED CHERRIES

SERVES **8**
PREPARATION **30 MINUTES + 1 DAY DRAINING FOR THE LABNEH**   COOKING **1 HOUR**

MERINGUES
6 free-range egg whites
330 g (11½ oz/1½ cups) caster
  (superfine) sugar
2 tablespoons cornflour (cornstarch)
1½ teaspoons white vinegar

SWEET LABNEH
500 g (1 lb 2 oz/2 cups) creamy
  Greek-style yoghurt
1 tablespoon icing (confectioners') sugar
1 teaspoon vanilla paste

POACHED CHERRIES
220 g (7¾ oz/1 cup) caster (superfine)
  sugar
1 cinnamon stick
2 star anise
500 g (1 lb 2 oz) fresh cherries, pitted

To make the sweet labneh, lay a piece of muslin (cheesecloth) in a bowl. Tip the yoghurt into the bowl. Gather up the sides of the muslin and tie together with kitchen string. Place the cloth-wrapped yoghurt in a sieve, then set the sieve over the bowl. Now put the whole thing in the fridge and leave to drain overnight. After a day, discard the liquid in the bowl. Peel away the cloth, then place the labneh in a clean bowl and stir the icing sugar and vanilla paste through. Refrigerate until required; it will keep for up to 1 week.

To make the meringues, preheat the oven to 120°C (235°F); line a large flat baking tray with baking paper. Using an electric mixer on high speed, beat the egg whites in a clean bowl until stiff peaks form. Add the sugar 1 tablespoon at a time, whisking for 30 seconds before adding more. Once all the sugar is added, whisk for a further 6 minutes, or until the meringue is firm and glossy. Add the cornflour and vinegar, scrape down the side of the bowl, then whisk for a further 2 minutes.

Now make eight little meringue nests, about 10 cm (4 inches) wide, on the baking tray, leaving space in between to allow for spreading, and using a few heaped tablespoons for each nest. Bake for 1 hour. Turn the oven off and allow the pavlovas to cool completely in the oven.

For the cherries, put the sugar, cinnamon and star anise in a pan with 250 ml (9 fl oz/1 cup) water. Bring to the boil, reduce the heat and simmer for 5 minutes. Add the cherries and cook for 7 minutes, then remove from the liquid. Keep simmering the liquid for 10–15 minutes, or until reduced to a syrup. Put the cherries back and leave to cool.

To serve, top the baby pavlova shells with the sweetened labneh, then some poached cherries and a drizzle of their syrup.

> *My Pa used to make these pies, although he used gramma rather than pumpkin, because that's what grew abundantly in his garden. I have fond memories of his old flour-dusted Baltic pine kitchen table, and the wood-fired oven he baked his pies in. He would always save the best-looking pie for us, and we'd drive home with it wrapped up in a tea towel, sitting on the back windowsill of our old Leyland, with the delightful smell of sweet, sugary pastry and aromatic pumpkin filling the whole car. We make this pie to sell in our stores on Thanksgiving Day.*

PUMPKIN PIE

MAKES **1 X 26 CM (10½ INCH) PIE**: SERVES **8**
PREPARATION **30 MINUTES**   COOKING **1¼ HOURS**

500 g (1 lb 2 oz) gingersnap biscuits (cookies)
200 g (7 oz) unsalted butter, melted
thick whipped cream, to serve
freshly grated nutmeg, for sprinkling
maple syrup, for drizzling

FOR THE FILLING
185 g (6½ oz/1 cup) light brown sugar
3 free-range eggs
1 teaspoon ground cinnamon
1 teaspoon freshly grated nutmeg
pinch of ground cloves
375 g (13 oz/1½ cups) puréed cooked pumpkin (winter squash)
300 ml (10½ fl oz) thickened (whipping) cream, whipped to light peaks

Preheat the oven to 180°C (350°F).

Place the biscuits in a food processor and blend into fine crumbs. Add the butter and blend until combined.

Press the mixture into the base and sides of a greased 26 cm (10½ inch) loose-based flan (tart) tin. Bake for 10–15 minutes, or until the crumb mixture has set. Remove from the oven and leave to cool slightly while making the filling. Turn the oven temperature down to 160°C (315°F).

Using an electric mixer, beat together the sugar, eggs and spices until combined. Gently fold in the pumpkin and whipped cream.

Pour the mixture into the pie shell. Transfer to the oven and bake for 1 hour, or until the tip of a knife inserted into the middle of the filling comes out clean. Remove from the oven and leave to cool completely.

The base of this pie is super crisp, so when you're ready to serve, find yourself a good heavy chef's knife and warm the blade to make slicing easier and to give a clean cut. Serve topped with whipped cream, a grating of fresh nutmeg and a drizzle of maple syrup.

To finish an elegant meal, all you need of this decadent dessert is a small slice, with a dollop of thick cream, of course. You can either make little baby tarts to serve with coffee after dinner, or one big tart to serve as a dessert. If you want to really impress, sprinkle the tart with some edible gold leaf.

CHOCOLATE GANACHE TART

MAKES **1 X 23 CM (9 INCH) TART**; SERVES **12**
PREPARATION **30 MINUTES + 20 MINUTES RESTING** COOKING **30 MINUTES**

1 quantity Sweet almond shortcrust pastry (Toolbox, page 37)
edible gold leaf, or good-quality unsweetened cocoa powder, to garnish
thick (double/heavy) cream, to serve

CHOCOLATE GANACHE
350 g (12 oz) best-quality dark chocolate, chopped
1 tablespoon unsalted butter
320 ml (11 fl oz) thin (pouring/whipping) cream

Grease a 23 cm (9 inch) loose-based fluted flan (tart) tin. Alternatively, you could use 24 individual flan tins, about 7 cm (2¾ inches) wide and 2 cm (¾ inch) deep.

On a lightly floured workbench, roll out the pastry to about 8 mm (⅜ inch). Press the pastry into the flan tin, then trim the edge. Place in the fridge and let the pastry rest for 20 minutes; meanwhile, preheat the oven to 180°C (350°F).

Line the tart shell with baking paper and fill with baking beads or uncooked rice or dried beans. Blind bake the pastry for 10 minutes, then remove the baking beads or rice. Bake for a further 10–15 minutes, or until cooked through. Remove from the oven and leave to cool. (If making baby tarts, cook the tart shells for 10–12 minutes; there is no need to blind bake them.)

To make the chocolate ganache, place the chocolate and butter in a heatproof bowl. In a saucepan, warm the cream over medium heat until it just comes to a simmer. Pour the hot cream over the chocolate. Mix using a hand whisk until the chocolate and butter have melted and the ganache is smooth and shiny.

Pour the ganache into the tart shell. Leave to set in the refrigerator for several hours for the chocolate to set; this tart can easily be made a day or two in advance.

Top with edible gold leaf, if using, or dust with sifted cocoa powder. Serve with thick cream.

Many years ago I read an article about the old-fashioned bramley apple, which has a distinctive sour taste, perfect for apple pies. I managed to find a grower and buy some dormant trees online, and we planted them at Essington Park, our home in the country. If the livestock don't get into the house garden and beat us to it, we make our pies with these apples when the trees fruit each year.

APPLE PIE

MAKES **1 X 23 CM (9 INCH) PIE**: SERVES **8**
PREPARATION **1 HOUR + AT LEAST 1 HOUR RESTING**   COOKING **1 HOUR**

375 g (13 oz/2½ cups) plain (all-purpose) flour, sifted
1 tablespoon caster (superfine) sugar
280 g (10 oz) unsalted butter, softened
125 g (4½ oz/½ cup) sour cream

FOR THE FILLING
8 tart apples, such as bramley or granny smith
50 g (1¾ oz) unsalted butter
110 g (3¾ oz/½ cup) caster (superfine) sugar
juice of 1 lemon
100 g (3½ oz) sultanas (golden raisins)
3 tablespoons plain (all-purpose) flour
1 teaspoon ground cinnamon
½ teaspoon ground cloves
1 teaspoon vanilla extract

TO FINISH
1 free-range egg
2 tablespoons thick (double/heavy) cream
2 tablespoons raw (demerara) sugar

In a large bowl, combine the flour and sugar. Work in the butter, using your fingertips, until the mixture resembles breadcrumbs. Make a well in the centre, add the sour cream and mix to combine. Divide the pastry into two equal portions. Work each pastry portion into a flat round disc, then wrap in plastic wrap. Leave to rest in the refrigerator for at least 1 hour, or overnight if convenient.

To make the filling, peel and core the apples, then slice roughly and place in a large bowl. Melt the butter in a large frying pan over medium heat. Add the sugar and let it dissolve, then add the apple and remaining filling ingredients and cook, stirring now and then, for 10 minutes, or until the apple has softened. Leave to cool.

Preheat the oven to 180°C (350°F). Grease a 23 cm (9 inch) pie dish. On a lightly floured workbench, roll out one piece of pastry to a 30 cm (12 inch) circle, about 8 mm (⅜ inch) thick. Ease the pastry into the pie dish, gently pressing it in and letting the pastry hang over the edge. Place the apple mixture in the dish, piling it up in the centre.

Lightly dust the workbench with more flour, then roll out the second piece of dough and gently place it over the top of the pie. Using your fingertips or the tines of a fork, press the pastry edges together, then trim around the edge of the pie dish with a sharp knife.

Whisk the egg and cream together, then use a pastry brush to brush the mixture over the top of the pie. Use a fork to pierce a few holes in the top of the pie to let the steam out. Sprinkle with the raw sugar.

Bake for 45 minutes, or until the pastry is nice and golden and the apple is lovely and soft. Best served warm from the oven.

Chapter Ten

CAKES

BAKING CAKES IS THE ESSENCE OF MY LIFE AT WORK. CAKES ARE WHAT STARTED MY CULINARY CAREER, AND ARE WHAT MANY PEOPLE STILL KNOW ME FOR.

Our big bakery in Marrickville, in Sydney's inner west, is the pulse of the entire business. It has been such a wonderful journey, from the first days of baking cakes in my tiny apartment, to watching large trolleys of wonderment coming from ovens so big you could hold a dance class in them. I marvel each day at their beauty, and I'm amazed at how we are able to keep the wonkiness and artisan approach even when we are making tens of thousands of cakes a week.

Imperfection is beautiful, I say...

This is the first cake I ever made. My friend Vonnie Gow taught me how to bake it one rainy Sunday afternoon. When I took my first bite, I thought I had died and gone to heaven — the biscuit base was so buttery, the cheesecake delicately melted in my mouth, and the lemon curd cut through the richness, balancing it all out so very beautifully. I was hooked for life. Nowadays we sell these in our stores and to airlines.

LEMON CURD CHEESECAKE

MAKES **1 X 23 CM (9 INCH) CAKE**: SERVES **12**
PREPARATION **30 MINUTES + RESTING + OVERNIGHT CHILLING**   COOKING **1 HOUR**

150 g (5½ oz) digestive biscuits
  (cookies), or your favourite biscuits
75 g (2½ oz/⅓ cup) caster (superfine)
  sugar
75 g (2½ oz) unsalted butter, melted
2 teaspoons warm water
½ quantity Lemon curd (Toolbox,
  page 44)
thick (double/heavy) cream, to serve
  (optional)
candied lemon slices, to garnish
  (optional)
sifted icing (confectioners') sugar,
  for dusting

FOR THE FILLING
300 g (10½ oz) cream cheese, softened
180 g (6 oz) caster (superfine) sugar
300 g (10½ oz) sour cream
3 large free-range eggs
zest and juice of 1 lemon

Grease the base of a 23 cm (9 inch) spring-form cake tin. Line the base and side with baking paper.

Break the biscuits into bits and place in a food processor. Blend until smooth, and the consistency of sand, then tip into a bowl. Add the sugar, melted butter and water and mix until all the crumbs are damp with the butter, like wet sand. Using the back of a metal spoon, and a straight-sided glass, press the crumb mixture into the base of the tin. Place in the refrigerator to set for an hour or so.

When you're ready to bake, preheat the oven to 150°C (300°F).

To make the filling, beat the cream cheese and sugar in a bowl, using an electric mixer, until soft and well combined. Add the sour cream and beat on slow speed to combine — don't overbeat the mixture, or beat it too fast, as this will cause the cheesecake to rise during cooking, then crack as it is cooling down; always have the speed set to slow to medium. Add the eggs one at a time, beating in each one until incorporated. Add the lemon zest and juice and beat slowly for about a minute.

Pour the mixture over the biscuit base. Bake for 1 hour, or until the cheesecake is a light golden colour, but still a bit wobbly in the middle. Leave to cool in the oven with the door ajar.

Refrigerate for 12 hours, or overnight, until chilled. Just before serving, spread with most of the lemon curd. Decorate with big dollops of thick cream and candied lemon slices, if desired. Drizzle with the remaining lemon curd, dust with icing sugar and serve.

I found a version of this lovely moist, summery cake in an old Vogue Entertaining magazine. It would make a wonderful wedding cake as it looks so fresh and pretty. You could layer the cake with sliced banana, rather than mango — or a bit of both!

HUMMINGBIRD CAKE WITH FRESH MANGO & FLAKED COCONUT

MAKES **1 LAYERED 23 CM (9 INCH) CAKE**; SERVES **12–16**
PREPARATION **30 MINUTES + 15 MINUTES ICING** COOKING **40 MINUTES**

3 free-range eggs
300 ml (10½ fl oz) vegetable oil
1 teaspoon vanilla extract
400 g (14 oz/2⅔ cups) plain
  (all-purpose) flour
1 teaspoon bicarbonate of soda
  (baking soda)
2 teaspoons baking powder
½ teaspoon sea salt
2 teaspoons ground cinnamon
300 g (10½ oz) caster (superfine) sugar
115 g (4 oz/1 cup) walnuts, toasted and
  chopped
300 g (10½ oz/2 cups, firmly packed)
  grated carrot
280 g (10 oz) tinned crushed pineapple,
  plus the juice

TO FINISH THE CAKE
4 quantities Cream cheese icing
  (Toolbox, page 46)
2 mangoes, flesh peeled and sliced,
  plus extra slices to garnish
100 g (3½ oz) flaked coconut or
  shredded coconut
sifted icing (confectioners') sugar,
  for dusting

Preheat the oven to 170°C (325°F). Grease two 23 cm (9 inch) cake tins and line the base with baking paper.

In a large bowl, beat the eggs, vegetable oil and vanilla until combined, using an electric mixer.

Into a separate bowl, sift the flour, bicarbonate of soda, baking powder, salt and cinnamon. Mix the sugar and walnuts through, then add to the egg mixture and beat well. Add the carrot, crushed pineapple and the pineapple juice, folding through until totally incorporated.

Pour the batter into each cake tin, dividing the mixture evenly. Bake for 40 minutes, or until a skewer inserted into the middle of the cakes comes out clean. Remove from the oven and leave to cool slightly, before turning out of the tins.

If your cakes have domed up in the middle, use a large serrated knife to cut the top off them, to give a flat surface. Place one cake on a cake stand or flat plate. Spread a thick layer of cream cheese icing over the top, then cover with mango slices. Top with the second cake, making sure it is on as straight as possible.

Spread the remaining cream cheese icing on top of the cake. Working your way down with a spatula, cover the top and all around the side. Gently press the coconut all around the side of the cake. Keep refrigerated until required; the cake can be assembled a day ahead.

Decorate with extra mango slices and a dusting of icing sugar just before serving.

> *With so many people intolerant to flour these days, it gives me great pleasure to bake and serve this flour-free cake seven days a week. I really love how it's crunchy on the outside, and all gooey and yummy on the inside. We almost always serve it with fresh plump raspberries and thick cream.*

FLOURLESS CHOCOLATE CAKE

MAKES **1 X 23 CM (9 INCH) CAKE**; SERVES **12**
PREPARATION **30 MINUTES**   COOKING **50 MINUTES**

250 g (9 oz) unsalted butter
300 g (10½ oz) best-quality dark
  chocolate, chopped
5 free-range eggs, separated
250 g (9 oz) caster (superfine) sugar
125 g (4½ oz/1¼ cups) almond meal
sifted good-quality unsweetened
  cocoa powder, for sprinkling
fresh raspberries, to serve
unsprayed rose petals, to garnish
  (optional)
thick (double/heavy) cream, to serve

Preheat the oven to 160°C (315°F). Grease a 23 cm (9 inch) spring-form cake tin and line the base with baking paper.

Melt the butter in a saucepan over medium heat. Simmer for about 3–5 minutes, or until the butter has clarified; you will know it is ready when all the solids have cooked off, and you are left with a nutty, deep-golden oil. Add the chocolate and mix until the chocolate has melted. Remove from the heat, then whisk in the egg yolks.

In a clean bowl, whisk the egg whites using an electric mixer until soft peaks form.

To the chocolate mixture, add the sugar and almond meal, mixing well. Fold the egg whites through, then pour the mixture into the cake tin.

Bake for 40 minutes, or until a skewer inserted into the middle of the cake comes out clean. Remove from the oven and leave to cool in the tin, then refrigerate until required. This cake has a great life span — it can be made up to 1 week in advance.

Just before serving, dust with cocoa powder, then garnish with raspberries and rose petals, if desired. Serve with thick cream.

> *Making the crepes for this spectacular cake is something I really enjoy. I always put my hand up to go on crepe duty, as it's a bit like a meditation — juggling two pans on the go at a time, in with the batter, flipping and tossing, then sliding the pretty lacy crepes onto a plate, stacking them up like a tower... It gives me a great sense of achievement, and also takes me back to when I was a kid and we'd have crepes with lemon and sugar on Sunday nights as a treat.*

CREPE CAKE WITH HAZELNUT & CHOCOLATE CREAM

SERVES **12**
PREPARATION **15 MINUTES + 20 MINUTES RESTING + 20 MINUTES ASSEMBLING**
COOKING **1¼ HOURS**

CREPES
300 g (10½ oz/2 cups) plain
   (all-purpose) flour
2 large free-range eggs
500 ml (17 fl oz/2 cups) milk
4 tablespoons butter, melted
vegetable oil spray

FOR THE CREPES

Place a damp folded tea towel on the workbench. Place a heavy mixing bowl on top. Sift the flour into the bowl and make a well in the centre. In a separate bowl, whisk together the eggs, milk and melted butter, then pour into the well in the flour. Gently mix the batter, slowly pulling at the wall of the flour and incorporating it into the liquid until you have a smooth batter. Cover and leave to rest for 20 minutes.

Place a 23 cm (9 inch) crepe pan over medium heat and spray with a little vegetable oil spray.

Ladle the smallest amount, about 3 tablespoons, of the crepe mixture into the pan so as to get a very thin crepe. Gently swirl the mixture around the pan so it is evenly distributed and runs to the outer edges. Let the crepe cook until little bubbles form and the edges start to pull away from the pan; this should only take 1 minute or so. Using a spatula, gently flip the crepe over, then cook for 1–2 minutes on the other side, until the batter has set. Slide the crepe onto a plate.

Cook the remaining batter in the same way, oiling the pan each time, and stacking the crepes on top of each other on the plate. You should end up with 20 crepes. Once cooled, the crepes can be covered with plastic wrap and refrigerated for a few hours, for when you're ready to assemble your cake. The crepes are best eaten fresh, so it's best to serve your cake the same day.

FOR THE HAZELNUT & CHOCOLATE CREAM

Preheat the oven to 180°C (350°F). Line a baking tray with baking paper. Spread the hazelnuts on the tray and bake for 12 minutes, or until golden brown, keeping an eye on them so they don't burn.

Remove from the oven and leave until cool enough to handle; if the nuts have skins on them, remove these by placing the nuts in a clean tea towel and rubbing them off.

Tip the nuts into a food processor, add the sugar and process until you have a smooth paste; this will take about 2 minutes.

In a heatproof bowl set over a saucepan of boiling water, melt the chocolate. Remove from the heat, add the butter and whisk until completely incorporated. Add the cream, salt and the hazelnut paste and mix well.

TO ASSEMBLE THE CAKE

Layer the crepes on a cake stand or serving platter, using a spatula to spread 2 tablespoons of the hazelnut chocolate cream evenly over each crepe, before stacking the next crepe on top. Continue until all the crepes and hazelnut chocolate cream have been used up, finishing with a layer of hazelnut chocolate cream.

Garnish the cake with flowers, then dust with sifted icing sugar or cocoa powder. Cut into slices and serve with thick cream.

HAZELNUT & CHOCOLATE CREAM

270 g (9½ oz/2 cups) whole hazelnuts, preferably skinned

55 g (2 oz/¼ cup) caster (superfine) sugar

500 g (1 lb 2 oz) best-quality milk chocolate, chopped

100 g (3½ oz) unsalted butter

250 ml (9 fl oz/1 cup) thin (pouring/whipping) cream

pinch of sea salt

TO FINISH THE CAKE

edible flowers, to garnish

sifted icing (confectioners') sugar or good-quality unsweetened cocoa powder, for dusting

thick (double/heavy) cream, to serve

This ridiculously pretty cake is one I always include if we're asked to prepare a dessert table at a wedding, garden party or kitchen tea; it's also a lovely cake for a picnic. I love the shape of the bundt cake, and the piquancy the lemon and yoghurt bring. If you don't have a bundt tin, use a round 25 cm (10 inch) cake tin, or two small loaf (bar) tins. And instead of thyme, you could garnish the cake with lavender flowers.

LEMON & YOGHURT CAKE WITH GLACÉ ICING & FRESH THYME

MAKES **1 X 24 CM (9½ INCH) RING CAKE**: SERVES **12**
PREPARATION **30 MINUTES**   COOKING **1 HOUR**

4 free-range eggs
500 g (1 lb 2 oz) caster (superfine) sugar
zest of 2 lemons
2 tablespoons lemon juice
375 g (13 oz/1½ cups) Greek-style
   yoghurt
240 ml (8 fl oz) vegetable oil
400 g (14 oz/2⅔ cups) self-raising flour
pinch of sea salt

TO FINISH THE CAKE
2 tablespoons lemon juice
125 g (4½ oz/1 cup) icing (confectioners')
   sugar
fresh thyme leaves or flowers, to garnish

Preheat the oven to 170°C (325°F). Grease a 24 cm (9½ inch) non-stick ring (bundt) tin.

Put the eggs, sugar, lemon zest, lemon juice, yoghurt and vegetable oil in a bowl. Mix together, using a hand whisk or electric mixer.

Sift the flour and salt together, add to the egg mixture and mix until smooth. Pour the batter into the cake tin.

Bake for 1 hour, or until a skewer inserted into the middle of the cake comes out clean. Remove from the oven and leave to cool slightly, before removing from the tin.

To make the icing, gently heat the lemon juice in the microwave, or in a small saucepan on the stove. Combine with the icing sugar, mixing until smooth, then drizzle the icing over the top of the warm cake.

If making the cake a day ahead, store it in a cake tin. Garnish with thyme just before serving.

I'm so enjoying the renaissance of the sponge cake. Every Saturday morning in our store, I line up the sponges on the bench, spread them with strawberry jam and fresh cream, then top them with sweet strawberries. From the minute our day starts, the phone rings off the hook with people asking us to put one aside for them! This is an unusual sponge in that it isn't as light as some; it's more like a pound cake, but lovely and buttery.

VICTORIA SPONGE

MAKES **1 LAYERED 23 CM (9 INCH) CAKE**: SERVES **12–16**
PREPARATION **40 MINUTES** COOKING **20 MINUTES**

FOR THE SPONGE
4 free-range eggs, beaten
200 g (7 oz) caster (superfine) sugar
200 g (7 oz/1⅓ cups) self-raising flour
1 teaspoon baking powder
2 tablespoons milk
200 g (7 oz) unsalted butter, softened

FILLING AND TOPPING
500 g (1 lb 2 oz) fresh strawberries
1 vanilla bean
150 ml (5 fl oz) thick (double/heavy) cream
1 tablespoon caster (superfine) sugar
150 g (5½ oz) Strawberry jam (Toolbox, page 40)
sifted icing (confectioners') sugar, for dusting

Preheat the oven to 190°C (375°F). Grease two 23 cm (9 inch) round cake tins and line with baking paper.

Place all the sponge ingredients in a large bowl; using an electric mixer, beat together until smooth. Evenly divide the batter between the two tins, smoothing the surface with the back of a spoon. Bake for 20 minutes, or until golden. Remove from the oven and leave to cool in the tins for 5–10 minutes, then turn the cakes out onto wire racks and leave to cool completely.

When you're ready to fill and top the cake, hull and slice half the strawberries, keeping the rest whole. Using a small sharp knife, cut the vanilla bean in half lengthways, then scrape all the seeds into a bowl. Add the cream and sugar and whip to soft peaks, using an electric mixer.

Use a large serrated knife to slice off the very top of one of the cakes, to make it completely flat. Place the cake in the middle of your serving platter or cake stand, as the bottom cake layer. Smear the jam over the top, then the whipped cream. Top with the sliced strawberries.

Place the second sponge on top. Decorate with the remaining strawberries, dust with icing sugar, and serve within a few hours.

TIP: The great thing about this sponge is you can bake a few of them in advance, wrap them well in plastic wrap and freeze for another time. They freeze really well, staying moist for up to 1 month, and will thaw in no time, ready for your favourite fillings and toppings.

*Made with almond meal rather than flour, this moist, luxurious cake holds a
special place in my heart: I once made it as a wedding cake for some dear friends.
When I'm catering for a special occasion, I cover the cake with a white chocolate wrap,
although you could halve the recipe and simply cover the cake with the mascarpone cream
and serve for afternoon tea.*

MIDDLE EASTERN ORANGE CAKE

MAKES **1 LAYERED 23 CM (9 INCH) CAKE**; SERVES **A CROWD**
PREPARATION **30 MINUTES + SEVERAL HOURS CHILLING + 30 MINUTES ASSEMBLY**
COOKING **2½ HOURS**

6 oranges
400 ml (14 fl oz) orange juice
6 free-range eggs
450 g (1 lb) caster (superfine) sugar
500 g (1 lb 2 oz/5 cups) almond meal
2 teaspoons baking powder, sifted
edible flowers, such as rose petals or
    nasturtiums, to garnish

MASCARPONE CREAM

500 g (1 lb 2 oz/2 cups) mascarpone
    cheese
2 teaspoons vanilla extract
40 g (1½ oz/⅓ cup) icing
    (confectioners') sugar
500 ml (17 fl oz/2 cups) thin (pouring/
    whipping) cream

Preheat the oven to 170°C (325°F). Grease two 23 cm (9 inch) round
cake tins and line the base and sides with baking paper.

Put the whole oranges in a large saucepan and cover with water.
Cook at a rapid boil for 1½ hours, or until the oranges are soft. Drain
the oranges and leave until cool enough to handle. Cut them in half,
remove any seeds, then purée the oranges using a food processor;
you should have about 800 g (1 lb 12 oz) orange purée. Add the
orange juice and refrigerate until cold.

Using an electric mixer, beat the eggs and sugar until light and fluffy.
Add the orange mixture and mix to combine. Add the almond meal and
sifted baking powder and fold in gently — do not overbeat. Pour the
batter into your cake tins, dividing the mixture evenly.

Bake for 40–45 minutes, or until a skewer inserted into the middle
of the cakes comes out clean. Remove from the oven and cool in the
tins for 5–10 minutes, then turn the cakes out onto wire racks and
leave to cool completely.

FOR THE MASCARPONE CREAM

To make the mascarpone cream, put the mascarpone, vanilla and
icing sugar in a bowl and beat until combined, using an electric mixer.
In a separate bowl, whip the cream until soft peaks form. Gently fold
the cream into the mascarpone mixture. Cover and chill until cold.

TO ASSEMBLE THE CAKE

Place one of the cakes in the middle of a cake stand or flat plate. Pile 4 heaped tablespoons of the mascarpone cream on top and, using a palette knife, spread it to the outer edge of the cake. Place the second cake on top, then spread with the rest of the mascarpone cream, covering the top and all around the side. Refrigerate until the mascarpone cream is totally chilled — a couple of hours, or overnight.

FOR THE WHITE CHOCOLATE WRAP

To make the white chocolate wrap, place a large heatproof bowl over a saucepan of simmering water, ensuring the bottom of the bowl doesn't touch the water. Add the chocolate and let it melt, giving it a good whisk to eliminate any lumps.

Lay two 85 cm x 10 cm (33½ inch x 4 inch) lengths of baking paper on your workbench. Place 4–6 tablespoons of the melted chocolate on one end of the paper strip and, with a spatula, smooth the chocolate over the whole strip. Lift the two corners and carefully wrap the chocolate around the cake, all the way round. Place the cake in the fridge. Once the chocolate has set, which will take about 10 minutes, pull the paper away from the chocolate.

Repeat again, starting on the opposite side of the cake, working over the seam. Smooth out the new seam with a damp cloth. Refrigerate for another 10 minutes, then peel the paper off.

Garnish the cake with edible flowers. Cut into slices to serve.

WHITE CHOCOLATE WRAP

1.5 kg (3 lb 5 oz) best-quality white chocolate, chopped

Many years ago, my lovely neighbours out on the farm left a basket of freshly harvested zucchini on our doorstep — a friendly gesture that often happens in the country. The following week, it was '100 ways with zucchini'. Of the recipes that resulted, this was my favourite. Very 1980s, very 'now'.

ZUCCHINI & PISTACHIO CAKE WITH ZESTY LEMON ICING

MAKES **1 X 23 CM (9 INCH) CAKE**: SERVES **12–16**
PREPARATION **30 MINUTES**   COOKING **1¼ HOURS**

300 g (10½ oz) caster (superfine) sugar
5 free-range eggs
350 ml (12 fl oz) vegetable oil
1½ teaspoons vanilla extract
100 g (3½ oz/⅔ cup) pistachio nuts, chopped
80 g (2¾ oz/¾ cup) almond meal
650 g (1 lb 7 oz/4 cups) grated zucchini (courgette)
300 g (10½ oz/2 cups) self-raising flour
100 g (3½ oz/⅔ cup) plain (all-purpose) flour
1 teaspoon bicarbonate of soda (baking soda)
1½ teaspoons mixed (pumpkin pie) spice

CANDIED LEMON ZEST
3 lemons
100 g (3½ oz) caster (superfine) sugar

ZESTY LEMON ICING
½ quantity Butter cream (Toolbox, page 46)
zest and juice of 1 lemon
sifted icing (confectioners') sugar, for dusting

Preheat the oven to 170°C (325°F). Grease a 23 cm (9 inch) cake tin and line the base with baking paper.

In a mixing bowl, beat the sugar, eggs, vegetable oil and vanilla until thick, using an electric mixer. Fold in the pistachios, almond meal and zucchini.

Sift the flours, bicarbonate of soda and mixed spice, then stir through the egg mixture until well combined.

Pour the batter into the cake tin. Bake for 1 hour, or until a skewer inserted into the middle of the cake comes out clean. Remove from the oven and leave to cool in the tin for 5–10 minutes, then turn out onto a wire rack and leave to cool completely.

To make the candied lemon zest, use a zester to peel the lemon zest into long, thin strands. Place in a small saucepan, add the sugar and 300 ml (10½ fl oz) water and bring to the boil. Reduce the heat and simmer for 10–15 minutes, or until the lemon zest is translucent. Remove the lemon zest using tongs or a slotted spoon, then spread out on a tray lined with baking paper and leave to dry for 10–15 minutes.

For the icing, beat the butter cream until light and fluffy, using an electric mixer. Mix in the lemon zest and juice. Using a spatula, spread the icing over the top of the cake. Garnish with little nests of candied lemon zest, dust with icing sugar, then cut into slices and serve.

LAYERED CHOCOLATE & SOUR CHERRY CAKE

MAKES **1 X 23 CM (9 INCH) LAYERED CAKE**; SERVES **12–16**
PREPARATION **45 MINUTES**   COOKING **1 HOUR**

FOR THE CAKE
300 g (10½ oz) unsalted butter
100 g (3½ oz) good-quality unsweetened cocoa powder
360 g (12¾ oz) caster (superfine) sugar
400 g (14 oz/2⅔ cups) self-raising flour, sifted
1 teaspoon bicarbonate of soda (baking soda)
1 teaspoon baking powder
3 large free-range eggs
1 heaped tablespoon sour cream
50 ml (1¾ fl oz) vegetable oil

FOR THE GANACHE
150 ml (5 fl oz) thin (pouring/whipping) cream
150 g (5½ oz) good-quality milk chocolate, chopped

TO FINISH
6 tablespoons kirsch (optional)
400 ml (14 fl oz) thick (double/heavy) cream, whipped to soft peaks
400 g (14 oz) tinned or bottled pitted sour cherries, drained
100 g (3½ oz) fresh cherries, stems intact

Preheat the oven to 170°C (325°F). Grease a 23 cm (9 inch) round cake tin and line the base and sides with baking paper.

Place the butter and 300 ml (10½ fl oz) water in a saucepan. Bring to the boil until all the butter has melted. Set aside.

Sift the cocoa powder into a large bowl. Pour in the melted butter mixture and whisk until smooth. Add the sugar, sifted flour, bicarbonate of soda and baking powder and mix until combined. Add the eggs one at a time, whisking well after each addition. Add the sour cream and vegetable oil and mix until smooth.

Pour the batter into the cake tin. Bake for 45 minutes, or until a skewer inserted into the middle of the cake comes out clean. Remove from the oven and leave to cool in the tin for 5–10 minutes, then turn out onto a wire rack and leave to cool completely.

To make the ganache, pour the cream into a saucepan and bring to a simmer. Remove from the heat and add the chocolate. Stir until the chocolate has melted and the ganache is smooth and shiny. Let the ganache cool for an hour or so, until it is at a spreadable consistency.

To assemble the cake, use a large serrated knife to slice the cake into four even layers. Place one cake layer on a cake stand or flat plate. Sprinkle with 2 tablespoons of the kirsch, if using. Spread one-third of the whipped cream over, then dot with one-third of the drained sour cherries. Repeat to make another two cake layers, then place the last layer on top. Using a spatula, spread the cooled ganache over the top of the cake. Top with fresh cherries. Cut into slices to serve.

BANANA CAKE WITH PASSIONFRUIT ICING

MAKES **1 LAYERED 23 CM (9 INCH) CAKE**; SERVES **12–16**
PREPARATION **30 MINUTES**   COOKING **1 HOUR**

3 ripe bananas, about 280 g (10 oz)

300 g (10½ oz) caster (superfine) sugar

260 ml (9¼ fl oz) vegetable oil

3 free-range eggs

2 tablespoons sour cream

350 g (12 oz/2⅓ cups) plain (all-purpose) flour

2 teaspoons baking powder

1 teaspoon bicarbonate of soda (baking soda)

½ teaspoon sea salt

4 quantities Cream cheese icing (Toolbox, page 46)

pulp of 3 passionfruit, plus extra for drizzling

Preheat the oven to 160°C (315°F). Grease a 23 cm (9 inch) cake tin and line the base and sides with baking paper.

Mash the bananas in a bowl, then add the sugar, mixing well. Add the vegetable oil, eggs and sour cream and mix using an electric mixer.

Sift the flour, baking powder, bicarbonate of soda and salt into a bowl. Add to the egg mixture and gently mix in; don't overbeat the batter too much at this point.

Pour the batter into the cake tin. Bake for 1 hour, or until a skewer inserted into the middle of the cake comes out clean. Remove from the oven and leave to cool in the tin for 5–10 minutes, then turn out onto a wire rack and leave to cool completely.

When you're ready to assemble the cake, mix together the cream cheese icing and passionfruit pulp in a bowl. Using a large serrated knife, cut the cake into three even layers. Place the bottom layer on a cake stand or flat plate. Place 2 heaped tablespoons of the icing on top of the bottom cake layer and, using a palette knife, spread the icing out to the edge of the cake.

Carefully place the second cake layer on top, then spread with more icing. Top with the final cake layer, working the remaining icing over the top and all around the side of the cake. Decorate with a drizzle of extra passionfruit pulp, cut into slices and serve.

COOK'S NOTES
SOME HELPFUL HINTS I'VE LEARNED ALONG THE WAY...

BAKING PAPER

As you read through this book, you might wonder how much baking paper I use in a week, and the answer is bucket loads — and so do my friends once I shared my secret with them. I use baking paper to line my cake tins, baking trays and roasting tins, and even when resting my cooked meat dishes, placing some over the top before tucking it all in under a tea towel. This is the best stuff ever invented, and really saves a lot of elbow grease when it comes to washing up.

BUILDING YOUR SALADS

When building a salad with grains, pulses or noodles — what I call a 'heavy' salad — I add all the ingredients, right down to the dressing and some sea salt and freshly ground black pepper, before I toss. The less tossing the better, and be gentle handed, as your salad will start to break down as soon as you toss.

When I'm building a 'lighter' salad, say a caesar or tuna niçoise, I gently layer all the ingredients in the bowl, considering the colour and aesthetics of the salad, and ensuring an even distribution of all the different elements. I always serve the dressing on the side, so that if there is any salad left over, it will last beautifully through to another meal time, without turning soggy.

FRESH HERBS

I don't often use dried herbs, but I couldn't thrive without an abundance of fresh and fragrant herbs such as mint, coriander (cilantro), parsley, basil and dill for my salads, and to add a perky freshness and colour at the end of pastas, soups and braises. Plucking from a bay tree, and rosemary, thyme, oregano and sage bushes at my back kitchen door, lends foundation and depth of flavour to my roasts, braises and sauces. Even if you live in an apartment, you can grow fresh herbs in pots on a balcony, or even on the kitchen windowsill — and they look pretty too!

If you're not in the habit of using fresh herbs, and are more likely to reach for the dried version in the pantry, I urge you to give them a go and freshen things up. You'll marvel at the difference in the look and flavour of your cooking.

Don't forget to give your leafy herbs a good wash before using — it's surprising how a cool little water bath will bring them back to life in a matter of minutes. I always give my herbs a big dip in cold water, then store them in the fridge wrapped in a damp tea towel.

By the way, when you buy a fresh bunch of coriander (cilantro), don't throw the roots away. Wash them well, seal them up and store them in the freezer for when you make a curry paste or a Moroccan dish, or any other recipe calling for this fragrant, flavourful root.

NUTS

I use a lot of nuts, particularly in my salads and cakes, where I need a bit of texture and crunch, or a substitute for flour.

It's important to use the freshest nuts you can find, and to be particular about how you store them and for how long. If you have ever eaten a fresh walnut, straight from the tree, cracked out of its shell, you'll get what I'm talking about. Nuts go rancid and bitter very quickly, so they are best stored in an airtight container in the fridge, rather than in the pantry.

I always toast my nuts to freshen them and add extra crunch. Just spread them on a baking tray and bake in a preheated 180°C (350°F) oven for 10 minutes.

RESTING

I can't emphasise enough how important it is to rest your roasts and steaks before serving. During the cooking process, the protein in the meat tenses up, and needs time to relax after it comes out of the oven, so all the juices run back through and make the meat more tender.

The rule of thumb is to rest the meat for at least half the cooking time. When resting meat, cover it with a piece of baking paper and a tea towel, and apply patience.

While we're on the subject of resting, homemade pastry too needs time to rest, to let it 'relax', as we say in the trade — otherwise it will shrink during cooking.

SEASONING

'Season, then season again' is my motto at work, and at home. I can't imagine cooking a tomato sauce without using salt and sugar to balance out the flavours and natural acidity of the tomato.

Salt and sugar, to my mind, allow food to sing. My only advice is to season near the end of cooking, because the saltiness and sweetness concentrate and intensify the longer a dish cooks and reduces down. You can always add more sugar and salt, but you can never take it away.

Use your intuition, trust your tastebuds and season away.

INDEX

THANK YOU

I've been cooking for about 25 years with the help and encouragement of so many... too many to list, although I'd like to thank all the wonderful people who've worked alongside me: you know who you are.

There are a few shining diamonds who have come on the journey from the heady beginnings. Adam Wilcox, my executive chef, has embraced my crazy ideas and helped me grow into the big business we have become today. This book wouldn't have happened without the support of my very talented and dedicated pastry chef, Anthony Grace. Thank you for being my rock when it comes to culinary problem solving, recipe development and helping me realise my dreams. Courtney Reece, my friend and fellow cook, thanks for your hard work, moral support and foodie inspiration; thanks for all the new ideas and for holding me up and encouraging me through the tough times. Ivy Puterflam, for all your years of assistance and being there for me through thick and thin: your support has meant everything to me culinarily, professionally and personally.

I would like to thank my wonderful publisher, Corinne Roberts, who gave me the confidence to write and shared my enthusiasm from the first day I stepped into her office, always guiding me in a most respectful way.

The look and feel of this book was very important to me — it was Michelle Noerianto, my stylist, and Mr Wonderful, the best food photographer in town, Ben Dearnley, who made this happen. And I couldn't have done it without the amazingly talented Claire Dickson-Smith helping in the kitchen.

The creative team in the Murdoch camp: Jane, Vivien and Sarah, you are wonderful; and Katri, who made sense of my scribble, and Mishmash, thank you for bringing it all fabulously together.

To my siblings, Joey and Andy, the best cooks I know, for always sharing your culinary ideas and being there unconditionally. Thank you for sharing recipes and helping to test mine. I feel like the luckiest girl in the world to have you in my life.

To all the customers who have supported me over the years: the people who come into my shop, buy my pies in supermarkets, eat my cakes on airlines and allow me to come into your homes to cook for you — I wouldn't be here today without your support.

Published in 2016 by Murdoch Books, an imprint of Allen & Unwin

Murdoch Books Australia
83 Alexander Street,
Crows Nest NSW 2065
Phone: +61 (0)2 8425 0100
murdochbooks.com.au
info@murdochbooks.com.au

Murdoch Books UK
Erico House, 6th Floor,
93–99 Upper Richmond Road
Putney, London SW15 2TG
Phone: +44 (0) 20 8785 5995
murdochbooks.co.uk
info@murdochbooks.co.uk

For Corporate Orders & Custom Publishing contact Noel Hammond,
National Business Development Manager, Murdoch Books Australia

Publisher: Corinne Roberts
Editorial Manager: Jane Price
Design Manager: Vivien Valk
Editor: Katri Hilden
Designer: Sarah Odgers
Photographer: Ben Dearnley
Stylist: Michelle Noerianto
Food Styling Assistant: Claire Dickson-Smith
Production Manager: Alexandra Gonzalez

Colour reproduction by Splitting Image
Colour Studio Pty Ltd, Clayton, Victoria
Printed by 1010 Printing International, China

MEASURES GUIDE: We have used 20 ml
(4 teaspoon) tablespoon measures. If you are
using a 15 ml (3 teaspoon) tablespoon add an
extra teaspoon of the ingredient for each
tablespoon specified.

IMPORTANT: Those who might be at risk from
the effects of salmonella poisoning (the elderly,
pregnant women, young children and those
suffering from immune deficiency diseases)
should consult their doctor with any concerns
about eating raw eggs.

ISBN 978 1 74336 725 4 Australia
ISBN 978 1 74336 747 6 UK

A cataloguing-in-publication entry is available from
the catalogue of the National Library of Australia
at nla.gov.au

A catalogue record for this book is available from
the British Library